MW00345590

GUTSY

Get
GUTSY!

LEARNING
TO LIVE WITH
BOLD, BRAVE,
AND BOUNDLESS
COURAGE

NATALIE FRANKE

WORTHY
PUBLISHING

New York • Nashville

Worthy
Hachette Book Group
1290 Avenue of the Americas, New York, NY 10104
worthypublishing.com
twitter.com/worthypub

First Edition: August 2023

Worthy is a division of Hachette Book Group, Inc. The Worthy name and logo are trademarks of Hachette Book Group, Inc.

The publisher is not responsible for websites (or their content) that are not owned by the publisher.

Worthy Books may be purchased in bulk for business, educational, or promotional use. For information, please contact your local bookseller or the Hachette Book Group Special Markets Department at special.markets@hbgusa.com.

Library of Congress Cataloging-in-Publication Data

Names: Franke, Natalie, author.
Title: Gutsy : learning to live with bold, brave, and boundless courage / Natalie Franke.
Description: First edition. | New York, NY : Worthy, [2023]
Identifiers: LCCN 2022057851 | ISBN 9781546015468 (hardcover) | ISBN 9781546004820 (ebook)
Subjects: LCSH: Courage. | Conduct of life. | Self-actualization (Psychology)
Classification: LCC BF575.C8 F73 2023 | DDC 179/.6--dc23/eng/20230315
LC record available at https://lccn.loc.gov/2022057851

ISBNs: 9781546015468 (hardcover), 9781546004820 (ebook)

Printed in the United States of America

LSC-C

Printing 1, 2023

555 Baltimore Annapolis BLVD.
Severna Park, MD 21146

- - - - - -

Phone: 410-449-3100
Email: severnaparkbooks@gmail.com
Web: parkbooksmd.com

Tue Sep 5-23 2:03pm
Acct: 3245 Inv: 117214 B 01
Ciri Fenzel

Qty	Price Disc		Total Tax

9781546015465 Gutsy: Learning to Live wi
  1 27.00   27.00 a

	Subtotal	27.00
	a TAX 6%	1.62

Items	1 Total	28.62
(906/520083)	VISA	28.62

======== Frequent Buyer Status ========
Credit earned with this purchase $ 1.35
Total credit on your account $ 2.80
Minimum required for redemption $ 5.00

----------Card transaction ----------
(retain for your records)
Resp. : TRANSACTION APPROVED
Type : SALE VISA
Acct : ************8906   USD $28.62
Trans : 0112903
MID   : 000002151488   Batch: 259
Auth : 520083   PNRef: 434112498
Entry : EMV_DIP cvm:MSG
EMV   : VISA DEBIT
AID   : A0000000031010   TVR: 8080008000

CUSTOMER COPY

-- Returns require this receipt --

To Huey and Harlow—be bold, be brave, be unapologetically you. You are loved. You are worthy. You are enough.

CONTENTS

INTRODUCTION

The thought of writing this book terrified me.

I am no novice to fear. I have done a lot of things in my life that scared me—starting a business, bungee jumping off a mountain, moving across the country, getting a tattoo, going through brain surgery, and doing hundreds of my own injections during fertility treatment.

I even did one of those viral dances on TikTok once. It was horrible, mind you, but I did it...much to the amusement of the tiny handful of people who followed me at the time. If you were to look up "cringeworthy" in the dictionary, the definition would no doubt include a small hyperlink to that particular video.

However, writing a book about overcoming the fear of what other people think feels like my most daunting undertaking yet.

There is something about this subject matter that digs at a very deep and vulnerable piece of my heart. It is the very thing I have fought against my entire life. It is the very thing that years ago kept me stuck for months, unable to create or show up online as my authentic self. It even kept me from pursuing things that brought me joy.

Who the heck am I to write a book on this subject? I haven't conquered this fear so much as learned to live with it. Shouldn't a writer have put the struggle far behind her in the rearview mirror before stepping forward to talk about it?

Shortly after my first book, *Built to Belong*, hit shelves, I had a conversation with an old friend that clarified precisely why I needed to write *Gutsy*. We were grabbing virtual coffee, as one does during a global pandemic, and catching up after many years apart. She was telling me about her job, and we swapped stories about what our lives were like now that we had entered our thirties.

She asked me how it felt to finally publish a book after all those years of dreaming about it...and my response was, "Terrifying."

She laughed a little and then said, "That's the thing about you, though, Nat...You have never let a little fear get in the way. You do it scared."

She was right. That about sums me up. Despite all of my many, many flaws, I am gutsy.

No one, not even the voice of imposter syndrome that rages in my head, can deny that.

I started a photography business at eighteen with zero knowledge of entrepreneurship or how to monetize a passion. I googled my way through it. I made more mistakes than I am willing to admit. I looked like a fool countless times. However, I just kept picking myself back up and trying again.

I became a living manifestation of the Chumbawamba song: "I get knocked down, but I get up again; you're never gonna keep me down"—you can yell at me for getting that stuck in your head. I'm sorry. I knew it was a bad idea...I digress.

I went to college, paid my way by photographing weddings on the weekends, and when it came time to graduate—to the shock of many people who assumed I would get a safe corporate job—I set my degree aside and went full-time in my business.

Those around me were not afraid to express their disapproval, concerns, and doubts about my decision. They never saw my business the way that I did.

To them, it was a hobby, perhaps a profitable distraction.

To me, it was when I felt most alive—behind my camera, working on my own terms.

The uncomfortable truth is I had no idea whether I could cut it as a full-time creative. I was terrified that my business would go belly-up. I was afraid that people would snicker and throw "I told you so's" at me from the widest corners of the internet if it all fell apart. I wasn't defying general advice with an ironclad, guaranteed plan for success.

I was taking a risk. I knew that, and yet...I did it anyway.

I chose to bet on myself. I threw my heart and soul into my one-person venture, and it grew. It thrived and became far more successful than even I thought possible. I was booked solid for months, with clients that I absolutely adored. I had the opportunity to travel the world photographing the most important days in their lives. I was living my dream.

Then the depression hit.

Out of nowhere, it rushed in like a tsunami, crashing into every fiber of my being. It was not the first time I had faced it. My battles with mental health stretch back all the way to my fifteenth birthday. However, this time it was different.

I was far more isolated in this particular season of adulthood. I had left behind the built-in community of school and sports to work from home, alone, with only my laptop and dog to keep me company on workdays. Building a business in a culture of cutthroat competition didn't help either. I opened up to friends about it. They empathized with me about the loneliness of entrepreneurship.

Connecting with others who felt the same way was a turning point for me. It was a small glimmer of hope and a moment of mutual understanding that running a business could, and frankly should, be different.

Together, we co-founded a community called the Rising Tide Society that rapidly swept across the world—from one post with the hashtag #communityovercompetition to over seventy-five thousand entrepreneurs gathering in cities every month to share advice and offer support. Pain became purpose, and I discovered a new passion beyond photography—cultivating community.

Over the last seven years, I have continued that work of supporting other creatives and independents. Through good times and unprecedented ones, I have grown into my role as a mama bear for small business. This journey has given me the opportunity to connect with thousands of people all around the world.

And after countless conversations with business owners in all stages of entrepreneurship, I began to see similarities in the fears that they openly shared with me. Do you know the one thing that holds so many of them back from going after what they want? Do you know the thing that keeps them stuck and second-guessing or burnt-out from hustling for approval and validation?

Do you know why so many of them almost didn't start their business in the first place?

Other people's opinions.

These are the creative risk-takers and entrepreneurial trailblazers, and even they are not immune to this formidable enemy. It has become clear to me that the fear of what other people think destroys far more dreams than failure ever could.

It prevents brilliant ideas from leaving the realm of ideation. It stops hopeful souls from daring to veer from what is expected of them. It keeps dreamers from doing and holds the brightest minds hostage to spend their lives in the shadows.

I would love to do that...but I could never deal with all of the criticism.

I wish I could quit my day job and take my business full-time, but my parents would never approve.

I want to launch a podcast, but someone I know has already done it. Would they think I'm just try-ing to copy them? Would other people think that?

What if people judge me for doing that? What if I try, fail, and let them down?

The fear of other people thinking negatively of us is the fear behind many of the other fears you know so well. Think about it...

Are you afraid of failing or afraid of what people think of you if you fail? Are you afraid of success, or are you afraid of the judgment and criticism that comes from stepping out-side of your comfort zone and into the spotlight? Are you afraid of public speaking, or is it the eyes of an audience and the thoughts they may be thinking of you when you take the stage that scare you? I could keep going, but by now you can see the point.

Even when we push ourselves past the point of hesitation and go after what we want in spite of the fear, we often still find ourselves hustling for validation and approval. We put more value in vanity metrics than we do in genuine indicators of progress.

We become captivated by the fleeting dopamine hits of

likes and comments on social media that remind us that other people approve of what we are doing in the world. We start to share not for ourselves, but for them—measuring our enoughness by double taps and tiny red hearts on tiny incomplete snippets of our lives.

When caring about what others think becomes an obsession, either knowingly or unknowingly, it stifles us. It feeds the monster of insecurity inside. Without even realizing it, we set goals for ourselves based on other people's definitions of success and strive to hit milestones that perhaps were never even meant for us in the first place.

We feel lacking when we believe that people think we don't measure up or when someone disapproves of our decisions. We stay silent to avoid criticism. We forget who we were before the world put its hands on us and the opinions of others molded us into a person we do not recognize. We hide our light to avoid drawing attention. We shrink and shrink and shrink.

If we aren't careful, we can wither away into a gray version of ourselves. Can you remember a moment when you felt that way? Leached of all color and life. Do you feel a little like that now?

If you do, I promise that you are not alone. It does not have to be this way.

Striving for what the world deems worthy means surrendering your soul at the altar of perfectionism. Looking first for external validation means putting your power and your purpose in the hands of someone else. As long as we are beholden to the opinions of others, we will always risk living lives that were never meant for us.

We cannot allow our fear of what other people may think to keep us from taking action. We also cannot allow endless striving for approval and validation to hold us back from living deeply meaningful and fulfilled lives.

This is not a simple challenge to confront. It is not a quick fix or immediate transformation. It takes intentional effort and oftentimes daunting introspection. Tackling this challenge head-on is going to require all of us to get a little uncomfortable.

Why might that be? Because there will always be some part of us, deep within our being, that is attuned to others' opinions (we will talk about the science of this in chapter 2). It is knit into the very fabric of who we are as members of a social species. This trait is not a flaw but rather a core component of our inherent design. It serves a purpose, although in our modern lives, it serves us far less so than it did our ancestors.

So while we cannot flip a switch and stop caring about what other people think of us, we can transform the way we understand and navigate it. *Gutsy* will show you how.

This book is the kick in the pants you need to stop letting other people's opinions hold you back and start getting gutsy. Whether you are launching out of school and into your first job, you have been climbing the career ladder for decades, you are starting your small business, or you are leaving the corporate world behind to raise your family, *Gutsy* will challenge you to define success on your own terms, feel confident navigating the world's criticism and expectations, and go after what you truly want in life.

Gutsy will remind you that your journey is for you and you alone. Everyone is entitled to their opinion. However, it is important that you remember that this also applies to you.

How you feel about yourself matters more than how others feel about you or what they think about your life decisions. So often we forget that. So often we let the whispers around us drown out the confidence within us. This is the moment that we unpack why that happens and become the heroes of our own story. This is the moment that we become the boss of our own lives and remember who we truly are.

This book is for the achievers who are tired of chasing after approval, the go-getters who are no longer hustling for validation, the dreamers who are done waiting for their moment to arrive, and the discouraged hearts who need a reminder that they are worthy and have always been capable of greatness.

We can stop the fear of what other people think from keeping us stuck, silent, and struggling to feel worthy. We can work toward self-acceptance, crank up the volume of our inner voice, and allow our core values to lead us forward. We can embrace the inevitability of one day making a fool of ourselves and even the potential of letting other people down. We can rewrite the rule book that we live by and chart a course for our life that is as unique as we are. We can shed the weight of the world's expectations and love the person we see staring back at us in the mirror.

Gutsy is a book written to empower you to do precisely that— to push past the fear of what other people think, a fear that so often keeps us stuck and stagnant, and to move forward with bold, brave, and boundless courage. This book is your road map to a life brimming with curiosity, confidence, and fulfillment.

This isn't a book about courage written through the rose-colored glasses of toxic positivity and stuffed with empty "pick yourself up by your bootstraps–isms" to leave you feeling up-lifted. When it comes to fundamentally changing your life, you have to be willing to do the work. I am not talking about effort that generates applause from the outside world or earns you the adult equivalent of a gold star. It isn't that sort of thing at all.

I am talking about doing the work that leaves you teary-eyed and uncomfortable. It is the type of deep intro-spection and brutal honesty that makes your palms sweat and your stomach churn. It is reflecting on the lies that you have accepted as truths and the people who fanned the flames of your insecurities by projecting their own.

I have fought hard to build a life for myself on the back of disapproval, criticism, and those who doubted my decisions. I have supported an army of others who have done that too. There is a way forward into the life that you want, and this book was written to help you get there.

Before we dive in, I want to share a few very important disclaimers that you need to know:

Although I am a psychology and neuroscience nerd who studied a good deal of the stuff in undergrad, I am not a mental health professional.

I repeat: I am not a mental health professional.

None of the content contained within this book is a substitute for therapeutic diagnosis or treatment. Always seek the advice of a qualified health provider with any questions you may have regarding your mental health.

My area of expertise is in entrepreneurship, community building, and coaching. I have been a small-business owner for well over a decade and for seven years I supported a community of over seventy-five thousand creatives and independents, helping them to push past their fears and grow businesses of their own.

A large part of my understanding of what courage means comes from the lessons I have learned from being a part of this extraordinary community. There is nothing "small" about starting a small business.

My experiences with motherhood and my rocky road to get there during my battle with infertility shape my perspective too. I've walked knowingly into my deepest fears, shared those journeys publicly, invited the world in for comment, and it has taught me quite a lot over the years. I am here to share those lessons with all of you.

There are stories shared within the pages of this book on subjects that may be difficult for some readers. I am intentional in my story selection and retelling to minimize potential triggers, but it is important that I give you the heads-up. These stories are from my own lived experiences and include topics such as depression, anxiety, a benign brain tumor diagnosis, infertility, and undergoing fertility treatment such as in vitro fertilization (IVF).

Just as there are parts of your story that have been unexpected, heavy, or challenging, I have dealt with that too. These lived experiences have shaped the way that I understand courage, and my hope is that you can see parts of your own story reflected throughout the pages of this book.

I am deeply honored that you have chosen to welcome me into your journey of learning not to care what others think. I do not take that decision lightly...So, earnestly, from my heart to yours, thank you.

I promise to keep it real with you in the chapters ahead. My greatest hope is that you leave this book with a fresh perspective on how the opinions of others have influenced your past and that you feel empowered to confront how they are holding you back in your present.

Enough about my story—it is time to dig into your own. Learning to live with bold, brave, and boundless courage does not mean living without fear. It means never allowing that fear to keep you from living your life.

Together, let's uncover what this looks like for you. One page at a time.

GUTSY

CHAPTER 1

GETTING GUTSY

I feel morally obligated to open this book with a disclaimer. A big, bold warning from a place of love that reads, *Good gracious, things are about to get real.*

Why am I telling you this? Well, I don't want you taking a big sip of what you think is sparkling water only to discover that it is a spunky gin and tonic, you know?

That happened to me once and it caught me completely off guard.

When it comes to this book, we need to be on the same page. You are about to be launched out of your comfort zone faster than my toddler into the toy section of Target as soon as we walk into the store. I am talking zero to sixty in under a second.

Think of this as a literary two-week notice—a declaration that you are done letting the opinions of others boss you around. You are ready to quit caring about the things that don't matter and fight for the things that do.

This book is a rallying cry for the ones who are tired of chasing after approval, hustling for validation, and bending over backward to meet everyone's expectations. It is a guidebook for those growing into their greatness—for the weary souls who are once again ready to be honest with themselves, take meaningful action in their lives, and carve out an authentic path forward into the future.

This book is more like a spicy habanero than a sweet bell pepper. It is zesty. It is fresh as heck. It is bound to make you sweat just a little. It will propel you forward like three extra shots of espresso on a Monday morning...which, as a caffeine connoisseur, I can personally attest will dust off the cobwebs in your mind and get your brain buzzing.

It may, in all fairness, also make you a bit emotional and introspective. There is truth in tears, and I have cried my fair share over the past three decades I have been on this earth. I am willing to bet that you have too. Part of unpacking the meaning of courage and facing down your fears over what other people think is being radically honest with yourself.

Here is what I need you to know right out of the gate:

1. Your definition of getting gutsy is unique to you and you alone.
2. Bravery doesn't always look the way that you would expect it to.
3. Courage isn't a competition. Comparison in this context is only a distraction.
4. How you feel about yourself matters more than how others feel about you.
5. You deserve to live a life beyond the limitations of other people's opinions.

Worrying about what other people think leads us to look externally for proof of whether we are on the right track or whether we are "good enough"—being gutsy means throwing all of the "shoulds" out the window and embracing your unique definition of success in order to find true fulfillment in life. There is no standard measurement of bravery. There is no single path to overcoming the fear of what other people think of you.

Don't be surprised when getting gutsy doesn't look anything like you expected. It rarely does.

For some, it means looking in the mirror and seeing the younger you within; it means speaking compassionately and honestly to that smaller self. Sometimes it even requires us to become the nurturer that we were hoping would protect our heart countless times in our past. Often it means that we must become the author of our own story—that we take the pen back from the commentators influencing our decisions from the sidelines and begin to write our future chapters ourselves.

In order to spring you from the quicksand of other people's opinions and launch you forward into freedom, we have to get *really* honest.

I am talking the truth, the whole truth, and nothing but the truth...so help me God! So, let's consider this first chapter as your official swearing-in ceremony.

This is an oath that you are making to yourself—a promise to be the undiluted, unapologetically earnest, and deeply vulnerable version of you. This is your moment to set aside all expectations of who you should be and commit to revealing the remarkable human being that you truly are.

And, friend, that oath goes both ways. I am promising to show up as my truest self too. There is no holding back, no gatekeeping, and no pretending that I have it all figured out. In the realm of self-help, it feels forbidden to admit that last part, but it is the most honest place to begin. I am a student of life, and this is a thesis after many years of grueling education.

Do I have it all figured out? Heck no.

Do I feel like I have an immense amount to share on the subject? That would be a giant yes.

I went from small-town photographer to the leader of a massive grassroots community of independent business owners in the span of a few months. With more eyes came more criticism, and my worry over the opinions of others spiraled. It kept me from wanting to show up as my authentic self. It made me second-guess every tiny decision. It nearly robbed me of the joy I felt in serving my community.

Perhaps *Gutsy* is more like a cookbook than an educational thesis in the sense that every day for the past three decades, I have been in the kitchen of life mixing up something new, testing it out, and learning along the way. Sometimes I got it right. Sometimes I didn't. The good news is that, at this point, I don't fear setting off the smoke alarm any longer. I just look at it as feedback and keep pressing on.

This is not a space where we hide our hardship or dismiss our struggle. This is the place where you are invited to the table precisely as you are. Your story is valid—past, present, and future.

For the next several chapters, there is no need to put on a show. In this space, you get to be the real you and throw all polished pretenses out the window. Here, we welcome messy attempts, embarrassing outcomes, and epic fails. You aimed for the goal and you missed...So what? There is no shame in showing up and giving it your best shot. Whether a glorious victory or a mortifying mistake—I believe you are more likely to regret what could have been than you are to regret failing in the pursuit of your wildest dreams.

Here, we show up, we step up, and we surrender our insecurities. I am talking about rolling up to the party with spit-up on your shirt and dog poop on your shoes (*which I have once done quite literally*) without worrying about a thing.

You hoped you would be further along by now? You are

not alone. Here, it is okay to grieve where you had hoped to be while creating space for new beginnings. Here, we honor the journey, the hardships you have endured, and the hopes you have yet to see fulfilled. From this moment on, you can stop sprinting to keep up with someone else's timeline and step forward purposefully, in confidence, onto the path paved uniquely for you.

We aren't competing against anyone here. There is nothing to measure up to, no milestones you have to prove you have achieved. You can take the world's expectations, drop them in the nearest garbage bin, and holler for me to take it out to the curb.

Here, we don't have to hide who we are or who we desire to become. You can reveal the most authentic version of yourself—messy, imperfect, and earnest. Here, there is no such thing as being too much or too little. Here, you are always enough.

Remember: no one ever changed the world by dimming their light, shrinking back, or avoiding criticism. Sure, it is safer to stay put, stay quiet, and stay stuck...but there is no gold medal for never getting started. Consider this your moment to uncover the audacious courage within yourself and make an impact on this world that only you can make.

I am your book big sister who wants to see you win... which means that I am going to tell it like it is. I am going to call you on your crap. I am going to push you to the edge of your comfort zone...and I am doing all of it because you deserve to know just how incredible you are.

I believe that you deserve so much more than a life of striving for the approval of others. You deserve to feel confident in yourself. You deserve to be empowered to use your voice. I want you to show up as your bravest self. I want you to turn every page with radical curiosity, audacious courage, and abundant grace.

The Future Is Yours to Define

It wasn't until I turned thirty that I realized it was okay to suck at something. Yes, I genuinely mean that. I realize that sounds a bit ridiculous, but it is the truth.

If you can't take the heat, then get out of the kitchen... right?

But what if baking brings you joy even if you burn everything that you put into the oven? Is it only worth your time if you excel at it? Are your joy, your curiosity, your passion not reasons enough to do something?

I spent the majority of my life believing that if I wasn't good or it didn't earn the validation of others, then I shouldn't do it. I never fully understood just how trapped I had become by wanting to please the world and earn some imaginary stamp of approval.

There is a good chance you are knowingly or unknowingly battling limiting beliefs precisely like this one. There are years of conditioning that have shaped your decisions and your perspective of what it means for you to live your best life.

Think about it...

Who defined what your best life is, anyway? Up until this point, have you ever stopped to think about why you envision success in the way that you do? Who painted that picture? Is it your original creation or was it slowly sculpted by the opinions of others and the expectations placed upon you from the moment that you were born?

If you have never tugged on the thread that weaves together your success equation, I am willing to bet that many of the things you think you should be and should have will unravel. What you do, where you live, who you call friends, how you spend your money and your time—all of it when examined through this lens gains new clarity.

Are you in the race because you love running or are you chasing after the applause and the fleeting feeling of validation you get as you edge closer to the finish line? Perhaps you are running because it is all you have ever known. Perhaps you never even questioned if running was optional in the first place.

The world won't fall apart if you slow your pace, stop entirely, step off the paved path, or move toward an entirely new destination. If you don't like the finish line that you are running toward, you have the power to change it.

It took me so many years of striving for the impossibility of perfection and simultaneously shrinking into the mold of who I should be in order to realize that it didn't have to be this way. And once I did...once the pressures and expectations unraveled, it required me to truly get gutsy.

Being authentically yourself is not easy. Going against the grain, speaking your mind, doing things differently, letting go of a path no longer meant for you—it all requires guts. It takes bold, brave, and boundless courage in order to move forward with confidence into the person you were always meant to be.

The moment you realize that caring about what other people think has kept you chasing after a life that was never meant for you, you have to get gutsy in order to move forward.

So, what does it truly mean to be "gutsy," anyway?

Gutsy (adjective):
marked by courage, pluck, or determination
Synonyms include "adventurous," "audacious,"
"bold," and "daring"[1]

I love a good dictionary definition; however, these definitions often have their limitations. I would be remiss if I didn't address one key consideration when it comes to defining what this term means to you.

Are you ready?

Here it is: there is no single definition of courage. No one else can tell you what your version of being gutsy looks like—not me, not your partner, not your best friend, and certainly not the honorable *Merriam-Webster*.

There is no one walking this planet today who sees the

---

1. *Merriam-Webster*, s.v. "gutsy (*adj.*)," accessed July 16, 2022, https://www.merriam-webster.com/dictionary/gutsy.

desires of your heart, the trials of your past, and the potential of your future like you do. Defining how this word manifests in your life is for you and you alone. It is a personal quest and an intimate journey.

Being gutsy sometimes means having the courage to start over, try something new, let people down, take risks, make mistakes, fail epically, look like a fool, be judged by the world, be misunderstood, apologize, lean on others, be vulnerable, and even be rebellious at times.

The more clarity you gain on what this type of plucky bravery means to you, the sooner you are able to set new goals in alignment with this mindset shift.

Your gutsy goals for the future might look different from the goals of every other person reading this book, and that's okay. I also believe that if your vision of the bold and brave version of yourself makes you a little nervous, then it is likely a very good sign. You are on the right track.

Gutsy goals may look like standing up for yourself, asking for a raise, ending a relationship, running for political office, or starting a small business. It could also mean finally getting a therapist, starting a blog, moving out on your own, launching a podcast, attending a networking event, or being more vulnerable on social media. There are an infinite number of ways to incorporate a little more courage into your daily life...and it will likely look different for every person reading this book.

Also, let me be downright blunt in this next assertion—

there is no need to read between the lines here. If the only gutsy goal you make is to look in the mirror and be honest with yourself, that is far more than many people can say they have accomplished in their lifetimes.

Step up to the mirror and see yourself with new eyes. Self-acceptance is a courageous act. Acknowledging who you are and what you earnestly want from your life is no small feat. This level of personal vulnerability requires bold and boundless courage for most of us. Here, we honor that.

I stand by my belief that no one else can define what it means for you to be courageous.

Think about it. If I asked a roomful of people to line up in order of who is the most gutsy to who is the least, how would they make that determination? Is a person's boldness or courage quantifiable or even comparable?

I'd argue that it is an impossible task.

The courage it takes for one person to bungee jump off a mountain may be the same amount that it takes another person to get out of bed in the morning—and I don't mean that hyperbolically. There are some of you reading this that know precisely the amount of courage it takes to rise from the depths of depression or keep going in the face of cataclysmic anxiety.

It takes guts. The world may value external indicators of audacious courage more than internal ones, but the latter are no less significant. The way things appear isn't always a true reflection of the way things are. Perhaps the inner work is the hardest work we will ever do. I know firsthand because

I have experienced all of the aforementioned scenarios. The depression, the anxiety—yes, even the bungee jumping.

Each of us walks a different road under different circumstances. What comes naturally to you might require intentional preparation and heaps of bravery for someone else. Something you have never had to overcome might be the very thing holding another person back.

Getting gutsy can look like saying yes or saying no. It can mean holding on or letting go.

We are most familiar with courage when it looks like going after what you want, speaking your mind, or taking bold risks...However, bravery can also look like being honest with yourself, asking for help, or taking a step back from a dream no longer meant for you.

You don't need to bare your soul to the world in order to be brave. You don't even need to take external action at all. You simply need to honor who you truly are in the comfort of your own heart. That's where the action matters most.

Most of the time, the bravest decision—the choice that requires the most courage—is the same one that the world might not understand, let alone applaud.

We also have to remember that looking to others as a benchmark for bravery is the very thing that we are trying to get away from. This is precisely why the lineup analogy is so important and so purposefully uncomfortable.

On your personal quest for courage, you are not being measured against anyone else. Their battles may not be your battles. Their strengths may not be your strengths. Their dreams, desires, and purpose look entirely different as well.

Other people are not your competition, nor are they your enemy.

The only person you are competing against is the version of you who cared more about being liked by others than about being your authentic self...the version of you who shrunk yourself down or dressed yourself up to be more pleasing and acceptable for the world.

There is only one thing that is more terrifying than being who you truly are and that is abandoning your authenticity and retreating into the person that the world expects you to be.

Is that a risk you are willing to take? To spend your life being a fraction of the person that you truly are? To surrender your uniqueness, your potential, your purpose at the altar of other people's approval?

Are you willing to get to the end of your life and join the countless others whose biggest regret at the very end of it all was "I wish I'd had the courage to live a life true to myself, not the life others expected of me"? Bronnie Ware, an Australian nurse working in palliative care, says that it is the unfulfilled dreams that were lost at the expense of others' expectations that is the most common regret of the dying.[2]

Are you willing to settle for that?

To join all those who, in their final moments when it is

---

2. Bronnie Ware, *The Top Five Regrets of the Dying: A Life Transformed by the Dearly Departing* (Hay House Inc., 2019).

already too late and their time is up, realize that they never went after what they truly wanted? They are held captive by the knowledge that if they had been courageous enough to truly be themselves, they could have lived a very different life. Do you want that to be your biggest regret too?

No way, friend...That is not going to be your story.

You deserve so much more than that. You deserve to look back with pride at everything you have overcome and every moment you chose to be brave in the face of what scared you.

You deserve to celebrate your successes and failures, to see your fingerprints on all that is good in the lives of those you touch...the ones who felt empowered to be themselves and pursue their own dreams because you had the courage to chase after yours...the ones who felt belonging for the very first time when you held out your hand.

You deserve to see this world made better by your voice, your gifts, your lived experiences honored by those who felt seen through your eyes. You deserve all of that and so much more.

Remember that your definition of what it means to be gutsy is unique to you and you alone. No one else can hand you the blueprint to your most courageous life, and because of that, comparison only serves as a distraction. Courage is not a competition. The way you live a gutsy life is going to look different from everyone else, and that is a beautiful thing.

Each chapter ahead is crafted to help you get over the most common manifestations of this fundamental fear. From navigating criticism to failing publicly, we're going to address the very things that often keep us up at night. With a heap of story-telling, a dash of science, and a sprinkle of reflective questions and prescriptive advice, we are going to walk through this together and emerge confidently on the other side.

In order for this book to truly shape you, we need to be partners in your progress. This requires you to do the work and ask yourself the hard questions. Questions that perhaps you have never been asked or never felt ready to answer.

True transformation can't be demanded of us. Our free will grants us the ability to stay stuck as much as it does to find freedom. That being said, when we do decide to commit to digging into the softest, most vulnerable pieces of ourselves and unreservedly embracing them, a new chapter of our life begins.

I am going to ask you a lot of guiding questions in the pages ahead. Only you can be the one to answer them. My biggest challenge to you is that you make the time to do it.

Here are some gutsy guiding questions to push this conversation forward:

- Why do you believe that the opinions of others matter so much to you?
- Who in your past may have made love and connection seem conditional, something you needed to earn, fight for, or that perhaps you didn't deserve?
- Who would you be if you hadn't spent years of your life trying to achieve the approval of others?

- When do you first remember worrying about what other people think of you?
- Where do you feel safest? Where can you truly be you?
- Where is it that you feel stuck? What decisions have you been putting off or where has fear been holding you back from taking action?
- How do you desire to feel in the future? What do you imagine the experience of success to be like to you?

Grab a journal, turn on some tear-jerking tunes or calming white noise if you need help focusing like I do, and get to answering these questions before continuing forward.

There is so much transformational goodness awaiting you in the pages ahead. Are you ready to get gutsy? Are you ready to stop living for approval and endlessly striving for validation and start charging forward with clarity and confidence?

I sure hope so. I really do. Let's turn the page into the next chapter...and what I hope is a new beginning in your life. Let's get gutsy.

CHAPTER 2

FEATURE, NOT A BUG

Stop caring about what other people think…is incredibly unhelpful advice.

It is kind of like telling someone to just stop sneezing.

Spoiler alert: it doesn't work that way.

You can't just tell your nose to stop doing the involuntary process it was designed to do, and "poof"—you will never sneeze again. There is a reason that your body responds in that way. It is designed to keep you healthy…and most importantly, alive.

This is also true of how we are always attuned to the opinions of others. You will, to some degree, always care about what other people think of you. This isn't inherently a bad thing (I'll explain the function of this tendency a little later); however, for most of us, it plays a larger role in our lives than we would like it to.

Sometimes what others think about us takes on more importance than what we think about ourselves. Even the most confident people struggle with this from time to time.

It can manifest itself in small ways, like influencing what we wear or what food we eat out on a date. It can also manifest in massive ways, like influencing the schools we go to, careers we choose, relationships we pursue, and even hold us back from taking any risks that might put us on the radar for other people's judgment.

Feature, Not a Bug

In the tech world, we have a saying—it is a feature, not a bug. This short turn of phrase essentially means that something operates the way that it does by design. It is not an accident. It is not a broken piece of code or a product oversight. It was intentionally created that way even if at first glance it seems like an accident or a problem.

And as odd as it may seem, worrying about what other people think of you is very much a feature of the human psyche. This tendency is hardwired into your brain. It is not in error that your mind works this way.

Why might this be? Well, for most of human history, our

ancestors lived or died based on whether they belonged. Being a part of a larger social group meant access to resources, safety, and survival. Being banished meant certain death. In my first book, *Built to Belong*, we dive into this concept wholeheartedly. Building communities for tens of thousands of people has only strengthened my belief that human beings cannot thrive in isolation.

As a result of that early human history, our brain has evolved to be highly self-aware of where we fit within the social hierarchy and to regulate our actions in order to maintain good standing in our community. Emotional intelligence and social cognition are highly valued human traits. Awareness of how others feel about us arises from that and is an evolutionary mechanism designed to mitigate the risk of being ostracized from the collective.[1]

Our brain understands that inclusion in our social group is a necessary requirement for survival, and therefore, it nudges us to modify our behavior in order to be accepted. If being excluded or disliked by others is unsafe, then it seems plausible that fitting in and being liked are the goals we should aim for...right?

You experience the impact of this neural hardwiring from a very young age.

Your environment and the people in it make it clear that

---

1. Benjamin Campbell, "A Neuroanthropological Perspective," in "What Makes Us Human? Answers from Evolutionary Anthropology," by James M. Calcagno and Agustín Fuentes, *Evolutionary Anthropology* 21, no. 5 (2012): 187, doi:10.1002/evan.21328.

there are expectations of who you should be. Every minuscule detail and nuance of who you are and how you exist in the world is thrown into the equation.

How you dress. How you speak. Where you live. What you like. Who you like. How you carry yourself through the world. All of it is added together in some fictional summation that we are told determines whether we are "good enough."

Little by little we begin to change who we are in order to fit the mold of who we are expected to be. The pressure to conform and strive for the world's impossibly high expectations begins before most of us ever even learn to write our names.

We are rewarded with praise for doing things that earn approval and punished for doing anything that brings negative attention to us or our caretakers. Slowly, interaction by interaction, we are molded into a version of ourselves that is more acceptable, more likable, and more successful in the eyes of the world.

Our uniqueness, bold defiance, and unrelenting courage are slowly stripped away as we begin to accept the false premise that we must be liked in order to be worthy. We become less of ourselves and more of who we are told to be.

Caring about the opinions of others is about as human as it gets.

You are not broken for thinking this way. It is genuinely and irrevocably a part of us. Our brains even activate the same neural substrates when we experience social rejection as when we endure physical pain.[2] Psychologists theorize that the overlap between social and physical pain was an evolutionary development to aid social animals, like human beings, in responding to threats to inclusion.[3]

Being shunned, judged, or ridiculed by others hurts like getting punched in the gut—perhaps quite literally, neurologically speaking.

You can think about feelings of pain like guardrails on the highway of survival. It keeps us heading in the right direction, which, in this case, is toward our final destination of a long and prosperous life. Your brain doesn't want you veering off the road into oblivion. Getting ostracized from the group, which is historically a very bad situation for human beings, is to be avoided at all costs...hence why we are so captivated by the opinions of others.

This is the feature. This is the way we are wired to operate. This is why you will at some fundamental level always care about what other people think. This feature, however, can manifest much more like a bug when our concern over the opinions of others goes into overdrive.

The same mechanism designed to keep us safe also has the propensity to keep us stuck. It slowly constricts our ability to

---

2. Naomi I. Eisenberger, "Why Rejection Hurts: What Social Neuroscience Has Revealed about the Brain's Response to Social Rejection," in *The Oxford Handbook of Social Neuroscience*, ed. Jean Decety and John T. Cacioppo (New York: Oxford University Press, 2011), https://doi.org/10.1093/oxfordhb/9780195342161.013.0039.

3. G. MacDonald and M. R. Leary, "Why Does Social Exclusion Hurt? The Relationship between Social and Physical Pain," *Psychological Bulletin* 131, no. 2 (2005): 202–223, https://doi.org/10.1037/0033-2909.131.2.202.

take action and turns decision-making into an exhausting feat of mental gymnastics.

When you are thinking about whether to speak your mind in a group setting, a neural network that psychologists call the behavioral inhibition system is naturally activated. This system enables you to assess the situation and weigh the costs and benefits of using your voice. Generally, when you have enough situational awareness, this network is then deactivated so that you can take appropriate action and move forward.

Research shows, however, that an abundance of concern over the opinions of others can keep your behavioral inhibition system turned on—thereby impairing your ability to take action.[4]

Second-guessing is exhausting. Holding back is debilitating. Constantly evaluating other people's body language, tone of voice, and context cues in order to determine what they may be thinking takes up an immense amount of brain power.

Think about this in a real-life setting. When you are unduly influenced by concern over what others think, your brain is running an endless cost-benefit analysis rather than taking action.

It is hard to speak your mind when your first thought isn't "What would I like to contribute to the conversation?" but rather "What will other people think if I speak up, and will I be judged, ridiculed, or reprimanded?" Likewise, it is impossible to try something new or make a bold change in your life when

---

4. Arthur C. Brooks, "No One Cares!," *Atlantic*, April 7, 2022, https://www.theatlantic .com/family/archive/2021/11/how-stop-caring-what-other-people-think-you/620670/.

instead of thinking, "How could this positively impact my life?" your default becomes "What if I fail and look like a fool?"

It is easy to see why our brain might be built this way; however, too much of a good thing can be a weapon we unintentionally use upon ourselves.

Magnified in Modern Times

These evolutionary adaptations are wired within us for survival, and yet ironically, in our modern lives they can prevent us from truly living.

This is due in part to the fact that we live in a far different society from the one that our ancestors inhabited and yet we are operating on roughly the same neural hardware. The way that we live, work, and thrive as individuals has changed in immeasurable ways, but our brain has not.

Evolutionary biologists believe that while our world has evolved rapidly in the past three hundred thousand years, our brains have evolved very slowly.[5] As a result, our brains are wired to thrive under a set of conditions that no longer exist. It makes certain features less applicable to modern life—ergo, we occasionally run into a wide variety of issues like this.

There are still circumstances in our world where having opinions counter to those in positions of power could cost

---

5. Nicholas R. Longrich, "When Did We Become Fully Human? What Fossils and DNA Tell Us about the Evolution of Modern Intelligence," *The Conversation*, September 9, 2020, https://theconversation.com/when-did-we-become-fully-human-what-fossils -and-dna-tell-us-about-the-evolution-of-modern-intelligence-143717.

someone their life. There are also situations where not adhering to a norm or being perceived as an outcast can result in catastrophic consequences.

Make no mistake. There is a reason why we care so much about how we are perceived by others, and there are instances where those instincts are necessary for our survival even now.

Fitting in comes with safety and privilege. Standing out comes with risk.

There is a reason why so many animals of prey have the ability to camouflage themselves in the wild. Blending in keeps them safe. Being seen puts them in danger.

The fear we feel about being judged or criticized is rooted in a very necessary function. However, when it runs rampant in areas of our life that are not going to lead to our demise, the feature itself becomes deeply harmful to our well-being.

Sometimes we have a fear reaction to something that isn't actually dangerous. In the case of other people's opinions, very often our body and mind react as if the danger is real, even when it is not.

Think of it like this: It is true that tigers can kill you. However, there is a difference between a living, breathing tiger and a guy dressed up in a tiger costume running around the field at a football game. Right? We don't need to apply the same caution to the second scenario as we would the first. However, sometimes we fail to distinguish when the opinions of others matter and when our obsession with them holds us back.

Modern life also means that we are less at risk of being

eaten by a tiger than perhaps our ancestors were. Similarly, someone's dislike of you today is rarely going to lead to the type of ostracization that will risk your life. However, it feels like sometimes our mind fails to get that memo.

Additionally, modern times also mean that we are living more public lives with more eyes on our successes and failures. Social media–fueled comparison fans the flames of our insecurities, and content bombards us with more opinions than any previous generation before us.

We have an inside look at what everyone else is thinking every single day.

Everyone has a platform to share their opinions. Everyone has an opportunity to comment on those opinions. It is like there is an opinion snowball rolling down a mountain and we are trying to outrun the behemoth that is hurtling down the slope behind us.

I believe that modern living puts this feature of our brain into overdrive.

New Software

So, how do we overcome this hardwiring in order to live boldly courageous and authentic lives? How do we acknowledge that these tendencies will always exist and still choose to move forward into the best versions of ourselves?

We have to rewrite the software that operates on our ancient neural hardware. We have to reframe our mindsets, learn new techniques, take intentional steps forward, and honor every incremental success that we have along the way.

In order to start living our lives with bold, brave, and boundless courage, we have to dive into the earnest depths of who we are as human beings. We have to uncover what is keeping us stuck or taking us off course in our lives, identify what is within our control to change, and build a plan to get there.

Oftentimes this means setting aside romanticized advice that leaves us feeling inspired in the moment and rolling up our sleeves to do the hard work of looking inward. Here are some ways to begin that process:

Leverage the Power of Attention

Redirecting your attention away from what you fear and toward what you desire is a powerful tool. While our fears do not magically disappear at will, we can control how much of our mental resources we are allocating to them. Intentionally pivoting our concentration from the opinions of others to our own inner voice and positive affirmations is a powerful practice.

Think of your attention like a spotlight, illuminating a certain aspect of your environment. When you shine the spotlight on your fears, insecurities, and the judgment of others, you are allowing those elements of your surroundings to take center stage.

By intentionally directing your attention elsewhere, you

are moving your mind in the direction of positive progress. If you can shift your focus, you can change your life.

Activity: Grab a piece of paper and draw a line down the middle. On the left side, write out the opinions that you believe others have of you. Focus on the ones that are rooted in fear, the negative beliefs that you worry others may think deep down. Once you have finished, rewrite those thoughts with something positive that you think about yourself. Flip the script and rewrite your own story.

Here are some examples:

FROM THIS:	TO THAT:
People think that I am too loud, bold, noisy, and opinionated. I take up too much space.	I radiate self-assurance, confidence, and strength in all that I do. I belong here. I deserve to take up space.
I cannot do anything right. Everything I try fails. I'm always falling back down. Surely people think that I am incapable of success.	I have the courage to persevere. Every failure is a stepping stone toward my future success. My resilience is my secret weapon.
If I quit now, people will think that I wasted too much time and have made a terrible mistake. They will laugh at me and think I am a failure.	I am brave enough to change my mind and strong enough to tackle any unknown challenge. My best days are ahead of me.

Recentering your own positive affirmation in the spotlight of your conscious awareness enables you to see the world with new eyes—identify sources of your insecurities, point out patterns of behavior that hold you back, and challenge yourself to reframe your thinking in a more accurate and confident way.

When you are trapped in the prison of other people's opinions, stifled by the need for their validation and approval, remember that you and you alone hold the key to your own freedom. You are the hero that you have been waiting for. Only you have the power to set yourself free.

And, friend, you owe it to yourself to be honest about what you want from your life. Your gifts, your passions, your lived experiences, and wisdom are not for nothing. There is purpose in the remarkable person that you are. No part of you is a mistake. You are uniquely equipped to leave your mark on this world...and my hope is to help you do precisely that.

By denying yourself the opportunity to lean into your purpose out of fear, you aren't only holding yourself back from living a life bursting at the seams with fulfillment and joy, but you are also robbing the world of the impact that only you can make. You are shoving all of the incredible parts of you deep within, locking it up tight, and burying the key far out of sight.

Honoring Younger You

So much of how we feel about ourselves is influenced by others' words and actions from a very young age. Although we can't change the past, we can rewrite the story that we tell ourselves in the present. We can shed the shame and insecurities that keep us begging for validation by rebuilding our confidence and self-esteem. We can hone and amplify our inner voice to propel us from the passive ruts that have kept us subdued or silent.

You have the power to be the hero that younger you needed. The only relationship beyond the spiritual that you will have from your first breath until your last is with yourself. It starts with you. It ends with you.

Activity: Think about a moment from your past where the opinions of others left you feeling wounded. What was the situation? Following our process from the prior activity, get a piece of paper and draw a line down the middle. On the left side, write the story as you remember it from the eyes of your younger self. Write about the hurt that you felt, the words that were spoken, and the opinions or judgment that has stuck with you ever since.

Once you're done, move to the right side of the page and rewrite that story. This will require you to look back at that moment with new eyes. How can you rewrite your perspective through a lens of self-confidence and self-love? How can you remove insecurity and self-doubt from the equation? Can the feedback be welcomed or the moment reframed through an adult lens?

For past moments that are harder to reframe or are rooted in cruelty rather than honesty, remember that pain is often projected. *Hurt people hurt people.* Someone's criticism or judgment often says more about them than it does about you. How does that change your perspective of the situation? Can you take the weight of that moment off of your own heart and let it go?

We cannot change the past, but we can rewrite the story that we tell ourselves about it. Healing sometimes comes from looking at old wounds with new eyes. Never underestimate the power of transforming your understanding of a prior moment.

And remember: there is no reason to believe that your future must look anything like your past. You are one decision, one conversation, one opportunity away from an entirely different future at any given moment.

This is a book about overcoming the fear of what other people think to live with bold, brave, and boundless courage. This is a story about the person you are becoming and the lives that you can impact when you have the courage to start by changing your own.

My goal is to take you from the depths of unhealthy striving, endless second-guessing, and exhaustive worrying to feeling confident in taking action regardless of the judgment or criticism that might await. The days of staying stuck and shrinking back are over. It is time to get gutsy.

This isn't the time to shy away from the good, hard truth. This is the moment you commit to fighting for your future and healing the heart within. The time you invest here, in truly getting to know yourself, will pay off in more ways than you can imagine.

Oh, and just in case you need a little reminder...

You deserve this—a life that you love surrounded by the ones who see, know, and value you for precisely who you are. Getting gutsy is about doing the inner work so that you can create the world you so deeply wish to experience. It is about living to the fullness of your potential and reclaiming power over your own life.

Leverage the power of your attention and redirect your focus from your fears to your bravest affirmations. Honor younger you and address the wounds you have been dealt at the hands of other people's opinions. Rewrite the story of your past and transform your trajectory of your future. All of this is within your power.

CHAPTER 3

REMEMBER WHO YOU ARE

In the months after my daughter, Harlow, was born, I struggled.

Heck, I more than struggled. I felt like a complete and utter failure as postpartum depression suffocated me from the inside out. It wasn't the first time I had battled with my mental health; however, it was the first time in a long time that it felt like the darkness was winning.

As maternity leave quickly disappeared and my return to work loomed on the horizon, it felt like I was running out of air. I felt the pressure to be everything to everyone—a thoughtful friend, a devoted partner, a selfless mother, an effective leader. I tried so hard to seem like I had it all together despite slowly falling apart.

It was as if the world expected me to be far too much.

Should I be learning to love my postpartum body? Or is it that I should have bounced back by now? Should I be excited to return to the job I love? Or should I be devastated to leave my little one in the care of someone else? My very existence had become a strange dichotomy of expectations that felt like they were heaped in judgment from the world either way.

I felt like I should be happy to hold this baby in my arms, happy to have completed our family, happy to be moving into this new season of our lives...and yet I was the furthest thing from happy.

The worst part was the shame I felt because of it. I had fought so hard to get pregnant—years of infertility, failed medicated cycles leading to IVF—that surely my gratitude should outshine the depths of postpartum depression, right? Surely, I *should* be happy.

Should...

Should...

Should...

There is that word again. The word that brings on the shame. The word that leaves us striving, never feeling like enough. Every time we say it, every time we even think about it, we pick up a heavy weight of expectations that were never ours to carry. Over time, the "shoulds" accumulate. They grow heavier, pressing down on us with an unbearable force.

I kept bending and bending under the weight of those

impossible, often contradicting expectations until something inside me snapped.

"Bend, don't break," they say...but I broke, all right.

Honestly, saying I "broke" doesn't quite do it justice. I burst into a thousand tiny pieces. It was as if a bomb had gone off inside of me and my confidence scattered like dust into the wind. I wanted to quit—to throw in the towel on everything, to retreat from everyone. I didn't even recognize the person I saw staring back at me in the mirror.

I was stuck. I was frozen in fear and unable to move forward. And one morning after crying from that painfully familiar pit of despair, my husband took me by the shoulders, looked lovingly into my eyes, and said,

Don't you dare forget who the hell you are.

At first, I remember thinking, "Wait, what the %@$*& did you just say to me?" as I blinked back the tears.

I didn't know it at the time—and it would take several months to see it—but this single sentence was the turning point that I desperately needed. My husband wasn't done speaking, by the way...He may be the quieter one of the two of us, but when he gets fired up, there is no stopping him. His voice continued on:

"Don't you dare forget who the hell you are. Don't you forget what you have overcome, what you have survived, what you have accomplished. Don't you dare forget how loved you are, how strong you are. Don't you dare give up now."

His words were like a flashlight turning on in a darkened room. His voice was a beam of hope in an endless night. He became a soundtrack on repeat in my head. Every time I paused, I heard his voice instead of the shame spiral that had been keeping me stuck.

Don't you dare forget who the hell you are.

It was that sentence that pulled me from bed on the mornings I didn't want to get up. It was those words that pushed me to reach out and ask for help. It was a spark of friction igniting into a flame of freedom. It was the catalyst that shoved me from the stagnation of that dark season.

Don't you dare forget who the hell you are.

Sweet friend, have you forgotten? Have you ever found yourself looking in the mirror and wondering when you became someone you didn't even recognize? Has it ever felt like you were so busy being everything to everyone that you merely forgot to be yourself?

When we spend our lives bending under the weight of who we should be, we risk losing sight of who we really are.

When we sacrifice our well-being under the pressure of surpassing expectations and winning others' approval, we risk losing the person that we have worked so hard to become. When we deny ourselves the help that we so desperately need, we risk losing sight of why life is worth fighting for. Carrying the weight of other people's opinions and expectations is often too much. No one person can be everything to everyone. All that pressure and the bending it requires us to do has a cost.

I am here to tell you that it is okay if instead you shatter. It is okay if you break and rebuild yourself from a foundation of core values and clarity around what matters most. Once you remember who you are, the opinions of others hold far less power over you. Once you solidify who you want to become, a better future feels all the more possible.

There Is No Shame in Breaking

If you drop something fragile and it shatters, it will be irrevocably changed. You can glue the pieces back together again, but it will never be the thing that it once was. There are some things that glue simply cannot fix.

Perhaps the same can be said about us too.

One of my favorite metaphors used to describe the beauty that can arise from brokenness is kintsugi—the centuries-old Japanese art of repairing broken pottery with a lacquer dusted with precious metal, like gold. It treats the breakage and repair of an object as something to be honored, rather than hidden or disguised.[1]

Oftentimes the pottery is more beautiful after it is repaired than it ever was beforehand. Golden rivers wind their way around the fragmented pieces, making them whole once again. I believe the same is possible for us too.

Two months after Harlow was born, Disney released the

---

1. Kelly Richman-Abdou, "Kintsugi: The Centuries-Old Art of Repairing Broken Pottery with Gold," *My Modern Met*, April 27, 2022, https://mymodernmet.com /kintsugi-kintsukuroi/.

movie *Encanto*. Due to the chaos of those first few sleepless weeks, I kept putting off watching it. It wasn't until the following spring that I snuggled up with my little ones on a Saturday night and turned it on.

In the movie, all of the main characters have different superpowers and face different challenges. One of them is the older sister Luisa, who is the strongest of the entire family and village. She is tasked with carrying everything, figuratively and quite literally, until it all becomes too much for her to bear.

The song she sings in that moment, when she feels herself on the edge of breaking under all the pressure she is feeling, absolutely wrecked me. I just sat on the sofa, my baby in my arms and my toddler beside me, with tears pouring down my cheeks. It is not a sad, slow, melancholic track either, but the lyrics themselves unearthed a feeling that I think you can also relate to:

Pressure like a drip, drip, drip that'll never stop...
Watch as she buckles and bends but never breaks

The weight of the world, all of that buckling and bending, is not how it is supposed to be.

I think we all know that deep down, but somewhere along the way we were taught that the worst thing we can possibly do under pressure is fall apart. I am here to tell you that isn't true.

What if breaking isn't the worst thing that can happen after all?

What if spending your entire life bending and buckling under the pressure is? What if chasing after perfection, squeezing into tiny spaces, holding back your boldness, and putting others' opinions on a pedestal are far worse than allowing yourself to fall apart?

There is no shame in shattering. Fall apart if you must.

Let the mountain of pressure crumble beneath you. Let the shame you feel fracture until it is nothing but shards at your feet. Grieve. Mourn. Scream up at the sky if it heals you.

Grant yourself grace upon grace upon grace. Find safety in the space where you land.

When the dust settles, rise.

Rise up. Remember who you are. Surrender who you should be. Pick up your pieces. Collect your courage. Onward, upward, forward you go.

Sometimes shattering isn't an ending but an answered prayer.

Sometimes a breakdown is a breakthrough in disguise.

The Road of Self-Acceptance

Self-acceptance is the foundation of a life well lived. However, you cannot accept what you do not acknowledge, and you cannot acknowledge what you do not allow yourself to experience.

How many of us overfill our lives in order to avoid having to truly address our own feelings? We pack our schedules, add to our plates, and take on more than we can chew—not just because of the pressure that we feel to perform, but also because the thought of having to be alone with ourselves terrifies us.

If our worlds stop spinning and our gears stop turning, we might be forced to truly sit with our feelings, and that can be a far scarier reality. I fall into this category, and the biggest lesson that I have learned in my unhealthy tendency to "go, go, go" is this:

You cannot outrun that which you always carry with you.

Your fears aren't this monster that is chasing after you. Your fears are the baggage that you carry with you. You cannot outrun them. You can only unpack them.

How many of us throw ourselves into helping others, unknowingly using selflessness as a form of self-avoidance? We commit our entire identity to being the caretaker, the supportive friend, the loving partner, and the virtuous volunteer. While a part of us may earnestly find joy in loving others through our actions, the far extreme of this behavior can sometimes be rooted in fear.

We give to others the very things we wish someone had given to us a long time ago.

Perhaps taking care of the people in your life has always felt easier than taking care of yourself. Addressing that pain and taking on a new role of being the recipient of care can feel uncomfortable and unsettling.

But let me ask you this—who looks after you?

If you are not doing it, then I am willing to bet no one truly is. The hard truth is that you cannot fix what you do not understand. When we deny ourselves the opportunity of truly knowing what we need, then it doesn't matter how much support we have in our lives, because it likely isn't addressing the underlying problem.

I could keep listing all the ways that we often avoid doing the good, hard inner work that we undoubtedly need. However, the most important thing is to make a change.

Sometimes this means giving yourself space to simply be—to exist precisely as you are in that moment. No striving, no analyzing, no working to change yourself in any way.

Sometimes this requires that you sit with your feelings, quiet the noise, and slow down the rapid pace. Sometimes it means silencing the world around you and perhaps even the thoughts within you, focusing all of your attention on a single point.

The simple act of narrowing your concentration to the rise and fall of your chest, observing the movement of air filling and then retreating from your lungs, can cultivate space for intentional stillness.

Don't be surprised if, as the whirling and rushing of the world fade away, you begin to experience feelings that you don't particularly like. Don't repress them. Don't run from them. Allow them to be.

During the pandemic, I was sucked into the fictional fantasy world of *A Court of Thorns and Roses* written by Sarah J. Maas. Those of you on BookTok[2] know precisely what I am talking about. Without spoiling anything—*I promise I would never dare do that to you!*—I want to share a line from the series that so deeply resonated with me.

---

2. BookTok is the nickname for the literary side of TikTok where millions of readers and authors share about books they love. It may or may not be to blame for my newfound obsession with reading fiction.

I am the rock against which the surf crashes. Nothing can break me.[3]

Tease me all you want for referencing a book about magic and fae in a conversation about self-awareness, but you cannot deny that this visualization is simply phenomenal.

When you start to feel that rush of emotions, visualize that it is a wave crashing up against you and watch as it retreats back into the sea. You are the rock. Your feelings are the waves. Let your emotions roll toward you, allow them to rise and fall, all while you remain firmly planted. It is downright beautiful.

It is important to allow yourself to feel whatever it is that you need to feel. We have heard that before; however, the part that so many people often miss can be unlocked by going one step further.

You are not your emotions. They are fleeting and fluid. They come and go. You, however, remain. Allow yourself to feel them. Bring them to the forefront of your mind. Only in acknowledging them can you discern the best path forward.

Strengthen Your Self-Awareness

When you set out to uncover who you truly are, you have to begin with introspection. You have to be your own advocate and expert. How can you do this?

Create a regular habit of checking in with yourself. Ask questions like these: When am I at my best? What areas of my

---

3. Sarah J. Maas, *A Court of Silver Flames* (New York: Bloomsbury, 2022), p. 621.

heart need healing? Are my needs being met? What has been bringing me joy lately? What am I struggling with the most?

- **Ask for help.** You are deserving of the support that you give others so freely. There are a multitude of reasons why it can be hard to ask for help, but it is absolutely essential. What resources do you need for your mental health? What tasks can you delegate or outsource? Who in your life can step in to help you personally or professionally in areas where you need it? What communities can you join to offer you the benefits of care and connection? Asking for support is not a sign of weakness; it is a confident sign of self-awareness and strength.
- **Set boundaries.** If it costs you your mental health, it is too expensive. If it steals your energy or robs you of your peace of mind, it is outlawed going forward. Boundaries are the barrier that protects you and the people that you love from harm. Start by visualizing and naming your limits—at work, in your relationships, in how you care for yourself. Set boundaries early, revisit them often, and be consistent in your communication of them.

Ask yourself, What do I need in order to feel seen, heard, and valued? What do I need to continue to rise into the most whole and nurtured version of myself? Focus on those questions and identify areas where you may have fallen short of honoring your own needs in the past.

Clarify Your Values

Another step in rebuilding a strong sense of self and a better path forward into the future is to clarify your core values. Understanding your values creates alignment between who you desire to be and how you are living each and every day.

When we strengthen our understanding of who we are, we fuel our ability to move forward with confidence. Often the inner turmoil that we feel or the insecurities that lead us to look for external validation come from a lack of confidence in who we truly are. The opinions of others hold more power over us when we are not clear on who we are and what we stand for.

I am certain that you have heard the word "values" tossed around a lot, but do you truly know what it means? More importantly, do you genuinely know what yours are? Could you list them?

Values are the deeply rooted, personal standards that profoundly shape every aspect of our lives. They are a set of key principles that indicate what we deem to be most important.

In the very first session that I ever had with my therapist, she gave me a homework assignment. It was a values-clarification exercise. If I am being honest, it seemed like a really simple task at the outset. I was perhaps a little too confident that I knew what my values were…However, when I sat down to complete the exercise, I found it took far more time than I anticipated.

What Are Your Top Five Core Values?

If you could only choose five values to live by, what would they be? This is the first assignment. I did you the favor of pulling together a list of fifty potential values; however, this list is far from exhaustive. There are values on here that may matter to you and there are some you will need to write in.

Achievement	Decisiveness	Honesty	Love	Responsibility
Adventure	Diversity	Humor	Loyalty	Security
Autonomy	Excellence	Inclusion	Optimism	Self-awareness
Belonging	Fairness	Independence	Order	Spirituality
Collaboration	Faith	Innovation	Peace	Spontaneity
Community	Family	Integrity	Philanthropy	Stability
Competence	Freedom	Intellectualism	Prestige	Structure
Cooperation	Friendship	Knowledge	Productivity	Truth
Creativity	Harmony	Leadership	Relationships	Vulnerability
Curiosity	Health	Learning	Respect	Wisdom

_____

_____

_____

_____

Values-Clarification Exercise

Step one: Start by crossing off the values that are the least important to you. Remember, there are no right or wrong answers—this is for your eyes only. Do any values stand out as something you know with certainty won't make your top five list?

Step two: Go back through the chart and circle the values that stand out as the most important to you. Which values are top contenders? Which feel most in alignment with your personal standards?

Step three: Review the circled values and consider whether there is a value missing from the chart that significantly matters to you. Add it in.

Step four: From this group of circled values and written-in additions, select the five that are most important to you. It is okay for this step to take a while. Refining can be the hardest part.

Step five: It is time to rank your top five. Create a hierarchy from the list—most important value first and continue all the way through number five.

Once you have created your list, take time to consider the following questions and evaluate how you are living out your values. Be honest with yourself.

Reflection questions:
- How do you live out your top five values in your day-to-day life? Is there alignment between these values and your behavior?
- If there isn't core-value alignment, where do you believe the inconsistencies are? What are a few ways you could improve?
- How are you going to implement these values going forward into your life? How can you make

them more visible or impactful in guiding your daily decisions?

Remember: having clarity and confidence around your core values won't stop the criticism or judgment from coming. It simply makes weathering those challenges worth it. It propels you forward with purpose and holds you accountable to fight for the things that matter.

CHAPTER 4

THE THING ABOUT OPINIONS

*Your ability to do awesome things is proportional
to your willingness to be criticized by people
who don't understand them.*
—JON ACUFF

I once made the mistake of posting a photograph of a fox in my local community forum.

"How cool! The elusive fox of the neighborhood," I wrote innocently.

What could possibly go wrong when posting a picture of a fox? I am so glad you asked. *Everything—absolutely everything.*

Almost instantly, the notifications sent my phone into an endless state of buzzing.

*"These menaces are ruining our community! Trap it
and relocate it."*

"Don't hurt the foxes. They are good for the environment."

"Isn't that right next to the elementary school? That's concerning."

"Are you a fox hater? What did foxes ever do to you?"

"I think that's actually a coyote. It is too big to be a fox."

"It looks rabid. I am calling animal control."

"That's Todd. I think we voted to name him Todd once."

"Animal control should be outlawed."

"Please stop feeding foxes. I know some of you do."

"Humans are the problem...Foxes forever!!!"

Within minutes, the comments descended into chaos. There were threads within threads of neighbors passionately voicing their perspective on foxes. Some loved the furry little creatures, others hated them, and some just posted funny GIFs as they watched the drama unfold.

A conspiracy theory even arose as to whether it was in fact a coyote in the photo and not a fox, with several people arguing about whether that species lived in our area at all.

Then someone posted about a reported coyote sighting in one of the local newspapers from a decade back and someone else discredited the entire publication, claiming that it couldn't be trusted. Obviously, that didn't sit well with a lot of folks. (*The jury is still out on whether coyotes actually live in my hometown or not, by the way. A general consensus has yet to be reached.*)

The controversial fox photo stayed at the top of the group feed for hours. Yes, hours. It was all anyone was talking about.

Neighbors jumped back and forth with their unique take on the situation as I watched, slightly horrified. By the next day, however, everyone had moved on to other passionate debates—parking issues, fireworks going off at 2 a.m., and folks not cleaning up after their dogs.

As quickly as the thread exploded into chaos, it was extinguished into irrelevance.

Here is what I need you to know. The thing about opinions is that they are everywhere, everybody has one, and they impact you on an even greater level than you realize. While we cannot control what other people think of us, we have the ability to be intentional with the voices that we allow to influence our daily lives.

This chapter is about deepening your understanding of external opinions and moving from being a passive bystander to an active curator of influence, one opinion at a time.

The Thing about Opinions Is That They Are Everywhere

We are living increasingly public lives in a culture of opinion overconsumption. Technology has taken external input and cranked up the volume. It is difficult to escape the barrage of thoughts that come barreling onto our screen from the moment we open our phone.

On social media, navigating the minefield of other people's sentiments is like a roller coaster we cannot escape. Keyboards have given everyone a microphone, and algorithms prioritize content that sparks conversation, ignites controversy, or retains attention.

Private thoughts have now become public posts. Words that were once whispered in hushed tones are now openly traded like currency for capturing fleeting moments of attention. Dopamine-driven feedback loops keep us scrolling and glue our eyes on a constant stream of what other people have to say.

This ultimately floods our feed with both the best of the best and the worst of the worst.

Then our fear of missing out, falling behind, or becoming irrelevant keeps us glued to our screens. We feel obligated to pay attention to the thoughts and opinions of everyone else—sometimes even at the expense of living our own lives.

We often don't see what is happening until it is too late.

We become caught in this endless cycle of striving for validation and monitoring external sources to tell us how to feel about ourselves and the world around us. One at a time, the hits of dopamine that we receive from the affirmation of others are like a drug that keeps us coming back for more.

Over time we begin to look externally to fill that increasing validation void within us; we surrender our self-confidence at the altar of other people's opinions.

Then when negative feedback is directed our way, the blow hits twice as hard. It pummels us apart—knocks the air from our lungs and the ground from beneath our feet. It leaves us reactively scrambling to pick up the pieces.

Whether it is petty gossip in the DMs, cyberbullying, or cruel comments on everyday content, rejection, judgment, and online ostracism can be deeply wounding. Yes, even when we aren't the intended recipients of those weaponized words or harmful actions.

It is easy to see mean comments on someone else's content and think, "At least they aren't saying that to me" before shrinking back into the safety of silence and scrolling onward to the next algorithmically selected scandal.

Even when it isn't meant for us, our brain takes note. We hold back, we guard our hearts more fiercely, we put up our walls, and we do what we can to avoid that ever being us. Those subtle changes, although often unnoticed or buried deep, can be harmful too.

Studies have shown that we vicariously experience embarrassment when observing other peoples' public screwups or mistakes. Even when we aren't the ones at the center of external criticism or shame, we still feel a small hit of embarrassment ourselves with or for them.[1]

Imagine the following situation: You are sitting down at a packed restaurant with your friends. Your waitress is running back and forth from all the tables, and it is clear that she has fallen behind on retrieving orders from the kitchen. While clearing a table, she piles all of the glasses and dishes high on her tray and tries to pick up the pace to get food to a hungry table of patrons. She takes two steps with the overloaded tray and trips. Glasses shatter on the floor. Dishes break. The loud smash is audible all throughout the restaurant, and everyone stops speaking. The room goes pin-drop silent, and everyone stares at her.

The way we experience embarrassment at other people's mishaps is a form of social pain. When the waitress attracts the attention of the packed restaurant under circumstances that are perceived as detrimental to her social image, the bystanders also experience a bit of embarrassment.[2]

Now, I want you to multiply this concept across all of the instances you experience on a daily basis when other people are publicly criticized or experience embarrassment online. The sheer amount of content you are consuming that activates this experience for you is astounding.

---

1. Sören Krach, Jan Christopher Cohrs, Nicole Cruz de Echeverría Loebell, Tilo Kircher, Jens Sommer, Andreas Jansen, and Frieder Michel Paulus, "Your Flaws Are My Pain: Linking Empathy to Vicarious Embarrassment," *PLOS ONE* 6, no. 4 (April 2011): e18675, https://journals.plos.org/plosone/article?id=10.1371/journal.pone.0018675.

2. Frieder Michel Paulus, Laura Müller-Pinzler, Andreas Jansen, Valeria Gazzola, Sören Krach, "Mentalizing and the Role of the Posterior Superior Temporal Sulcus in Sharing Others' Embarrassment," *Cerebral Cortex* 25, no. 8 (August 2015): 2065–2075, https://doi.org/10.1093/cercor/bhu011.

Perhaps in the past you might have experienced some vicarious rumblings of embarrassment when your waitress dropped her tray or a student was called up to the front of the room with a piece of toilet paper stuck to their shoe. However, today—between memes of embarrassing moments, sound bites that become trending audio, vicious comments on any article or post—we experience them much more regularly than in the past. You can begin to see the larger impact that this may have on how you choose to navigate the world.

Remember—your brain wants you to avoid pain at all costs. This includes social pain and exclusion. If you are inundated with vicarious experiences of embarrassment multiple times a day or witness others being shamed in the public eye, it is understandable why you might do anything in your power to avoid that happening to you.

When opinions are everywhere, the possibility for embarrassment is also everywhere. The sheer quantity of content we consume and the ability for everyone to share their judgment aloud set the stage for these fears to be dramatically amplified.

The Thing about Opinions Is That Everybody Has One

When I was a kid, I remember hearing about how opinions are like butts (all people have one and most of them stink), but I am a respectable professional and there will be no talk of that here.

Instead, indulge me for just a moment and imagine that opinions are like ants. Where one goes, many more will follow. One ant isn't that big of a deal, but when an entire colony descends upon you at a picnic, it is impossible to enjoy your lunch.

It was Elbert Hubbard who once said, "If you would escape moral and physical assassination, do nothing, say nothing, be nothing."

And likewise, it also doesn't matter whether you invited the ants to the party or not...If you step outside with a plate full of food and do nearly anything at all, they are ready and waiting to pounce. The only way you can truly avoid them is by doing absolutely nothing in the safety of your home (and frankly, even then they sometimes seem to find a way in).

A single leaf-cutter ant can lift up to fifty times its body weight with its jaw and withstand up to five thousand times that on its neck joint. They are considered one of the strongest animals on the planet.[3] If you had the same amount of strength as a leaf-cutter ant, then you could theoretically pick up a minivan with your mouth.[4]

---

3. Vienny Nguyen, Blaine Lilly, Carlos Castro, "The Exoskeletal Structure and Tensile Loading Behavior of an Ant Neck Joint," *Journal of Biomechanics* 47, no. 2 (2014): 497–504, https://doi.org/10.1016/j.jbiomech.2013.10.053.
4. United States Fish and Wildlife Service, "5 Fascinating Facts about Leaf Cutter Ants," FWS.gov, March 10, 2016, https://www.fws.gov/story/2016-03/5-fascinating-facts-about-leaf-cutter-ants.

Isn't that wild? Add that to your next game of trivia and watch jaws drop. I digress...

Metaphorically speaking, the opinions of others have a tendency to be an even stronger influence than you realize. You will underestimate them like the infinitesimal insect that they appear to be, and yet they will have no problem knocking you off your feet without notice.

Roman philosopher Marcus Aurelius is famous for saying, "It never ceases to amaze me: we all love ourselves more than other people, but care more about their opinion than our own."[5]

A famous philosopher and a metaphor about ants—y'all, I am really feeling feisty out of the gate with this book, huh?

What Aurelius touches on here is critical. We all have a tendency to care far more about other people's opinions of us than our own. Even when it is none of our business, we go searching for clues as to how someone else might feel or go seeking their approval to fill the void where our own sense of self-confidence should reside.

We'll get into the nitty-gritty of self-esteem in the next chapter—don't you worry! But before we do, there is more that you need to remember about everyone and their opinions.

The Thing about Opinions Is That They Aren't Facts

I am not trying to be a jerk when I say this. I promise, I'm not. However, it is critical for you to remember that opinions are

---

5. Marcus Aurelius, *Meditations: A New Translation* (United Kingdom: Random House, 2002).

not facts. That's not simply my take on the concept either...
That is what makes an opinion an opinion.

By definition, an opinion is "a belief or judgment that
rests on grounds insufficient to produce complete certainty."[6]
It can also be described as a personal view or attitude about
something.

A fact would be "the sky is blue." An opinion would be
"the sky is beautiful." We can't differ on the truth that is
inherent in a fact; however, opinions leave room for subjectivity and disagreement.

This is important because oftentimes when we hear someone hold an opinion of us, we can easily trip and fall down the
rabbit hole of accepting their assessment as truth. While opinions are often rooted in a nugget of reality, there is an immense
amount of individual perspective that is brought to the table.

One person stands quietly at the edge of a party. They
don't speak to anyone and leave shortly thereafter. If you ask
a partygoer what they think, their responses may vary. One
might say the person was rude and too snobby to interact with
the other people at the party. Another might say that the person was shy. One might believe that the person wasn't feeling
well because they are normally very friendly. The point being
everyone is entitled to their own opinion, and by definition
those opinions are not the absolute truth.

---

6. Dictionary.com, s.v. "opinion (*n.*)," accessed October 31, 2022, https://www.dictionary
.com/browse/opinion.

I studied the psychology of seeing in my undergraduate years at Penn, and it always fascinated me how two people can experience the same object and have vastly different experiences. They both have the same beams of light that enter their eye, the same photons that land on their retinas. That information is then transported through the optic nerve to the visual cortex in the back of the brain. There it is processed.

Your brain receives the information and then tries to make sense of it. As a result, your knowledge, past experiences, and even your trauma influence how you ultimately view the world.

We see not with our eyes, but with our mind. As a result, we all see the world differently.

Opinions are very similar. We can agree objectively on the facts and yet differ immensely on our opinions that arise from that information. One person may think the sky is indeed beautiful, but to another it may represent negative experiences and therefore be seen as something else entirely.

The Thing about Opinions Is That They Influence Us

"You sent a voice memo? Wow—how old are you?" my younger cousins teased in our family group chat. The snark is strong with this crew, y'all. You cannot get away with anything in my family. Someone always has something to say about it.

"I am sorry, what????" I responded with far more question marks than were grammatically correct. "You try texting with a toddler running around and see what chaos ensues. Voice memos for life!" I replied.

First Gen Z came for my skinny jeans, then my side parts, and now they want to outlaw voice memos too? Lord have mercy!

The truth, though, is that as much as we don't *want* to care when our actions or aesthetic are deemed uncool by others, most of us can't help but take notice. Each of us navigates this in our own way, and not everyone is influenced to the same degree.

The trendsetters are attuned to subtle changes and often leap before the masses. The mainstreamers are gently nudged to explore shifts in sentiment. The contrarians make it their personality to reject those trends entirely, which means that despite seeming to remain uninfluenced, they are just as attuned to opinion shifts as the rest of us.

Which are you? Or perhaps a better question is, Which do you believe that you are?

Opinions are persuasive, and they influence us even when we don't want them to. Most of us are reluctant to admit or even accept just how impressionable we are. Our brains are hardwired to encourage us to surround ourselves with people who think like we do and simultaneously limit any beliefs that go against those of our peers.[7]

No one is completely exempt from external influence.

7. Robert B. Cialdini and Noah J. Goldstein, "Social Influence: Compliance and Conformity," *Annual Review of Psychology* 55 (2004): 591–621.

We are all pulled and pushed by the forces around us. The opinions of others impact us on a deep, nonconscious level—most of the time we aren't even aware that it is happening.

If our stance or belief is in alignment with the point of view of the people who are important to us, our opinion is reinforced in the pleasure centers of the brain. Conversely, when our beliefs are in opposition to others or deviate from popular opinion, the brain signals that a "mistake" has been made and nudges us toward conformity.[8]

We use the reactions of others to help determine what is valuable. Daily decisions like what to wear or what to eat as well as broader mindsets like what to celebrate, what to fear, and what is trendy are just a few examples of what is shaped by the opinions of those around us.

Perceived value can be directly changed through social influence. The opinions of others alter a very foundational mechanism in our brain that reflects an immediate change in our values. Therefore, neuroscientists argue that social influence at such a basic level may contribute to the rapid learning and spread of values throughout a population.[9]

Being told that a voice memo (or anything, for that matter) is contrary to what is deemed "acceptable" by our peers

---

8. Liudmila Mezentseva, "Can the Brain Resist the Group Opinion?," Neuroscience News, February 8, 2021, https://neurosciencenews.com/social-influence-brain-17709/.

9. Daniel K. Campbell-Meiklejohn, Dominik R. Bach, Andreas Roepstorff, Raymond J. Dolan, Chris D. Frith, "How the Opinion of Others Affects Our Valuation of Objects," *Current Biology* 20, no. 13 (July 2010):1165–70, doi: 10.1016/j.cub.2010.04.055.

will change the way that we feel about sending one...even if we still continue with the behavior.

We might scrap voice memos and resort only to texting. Or stop using them around some people and send them only to those who wouldn't be aware of our uncoolness. We might shrug the comment off but think about it from time to time when sending voice memos in the future. The rebels among us might even double down and strictly send voice memos to prove a point...which I can neither confirm nor deny that I did in my family group chat.

We have also seen this in the case of denim trends in the past few years—or a recent moment in time that I have nick-named "the war on skinny jeans." At first, many of us collectively complained about giving up our long-held aesthetic. Then slowly we saw more stylish folks begin to wear wide- or straight-leg styles, and our fascination sparked. Stores began carrying more and more of the emerging trend. Fashion creators started churning out viral content that featured mom jeans. Several months later, many of us realized that we too have started to prefer a different cut of denim, and our skinnies are getting less and less wear.

It is the evolution from the "I would never wear that" eye roll to the "this is my entire aesthetic now" that plays out over and over again.

This happens frequently with colloquial language too. Words start popping up within specific social groups, the mainstream catches wind of them, frequency of use occurs, and over time, words and phrases are absorbed into broader discourse.

Words like "dad bod," "Fluffernutter," and "amirite" became so commonly used that they received official word status from the very dictionary gurus themselves: *Merriam-Webster.*[10]

Shared language builds trust, and as human beings, we have a knack for rapidly adapting to language norms in order to ensure that we remain in good standing with our peers.

When I jump on work calls with my colleagues in tech, you better believe I am going to circle back about getting alignment on our North Star metric so that we can continue to build a sticky product that reduces churn and increases our gross payment volume.

Was that a different language? Some of you will reread that painful wordy sentence a few more times to see if you can unlock the mysteries of Silicon Valley jargon. For others, you absorbed that immediately and felt transported into a Monday-morning Zoom call with your colleagues (*and I am sorry for that—truly I am!*).

Another way of looking at the influence of opinion is through the evolution of commonly used words over time. Think about how we describe something that is perceived as being at the cultural forefront—something that is desirable, popular, or even celebrated for being a bit edgy or on the fringe of mainstream.

---

10. *Merriam-Webster,* "We've Added 455 New Words to the Dictionary for October 2021," accessed October 31, 2022, https://www.merriam-webster.com/words-at-play/new-words -in-the-dictionary-october-2021.

Many colloquial terms have a finite life cycle of cultural acceptability. They are in...until they are out and collective favor moves on to something else. When the trendsetters stop saying it, slowly everyone is influenced to follow suit.

1940	1950	1960	1970	1980	1990	2000	2006
Swell	Hip	Boss	Groovy	Gnarly/Tubular	Rad/Dope	Wicked/Tight	Sweet [11]

In the past decade, we have experienced saying that something cool was "lit" to then being "on fleek" to finally calling it "fire" before abandoning words altogether and just using a fire emoji. Now, even emojis have relevancy life spans—some are fading in and out of popularity based on what they have come to signify in a cultural context.

It is hard to keep track, if you ask me...Nonetheless, many of you have traded your crying-laughing emoji for a set of skulls, and others are still blissfully unaware of the latest set of opinions on the matter.

The Opinions That Surround Us Sway the Opinions within Us

We are deeply influenced by the thoughts and broader mindsets of our immediate environment. Whether we are aware of it or not, whether we like it or not, the thoughts of those around us influence us greatly.

---

11. "A Brief History of 'Cool,'" *Fast Company*, July 1, 2006, https://www.fastcompany.com/57135/brief-history-cool.

Similar to the old adage "Show me your friends and I'll show you your future," I have come to believe that content is the contemporary version of this concept. If you swap in the word "feed" for "friends," it feels uncomfortably relevant... perhaps even like a personal attack if you, like me, spend a significant amount of time on social media.

Show Me Your Feed and I'll Show You Your Future

We become what we consume, and when we consume more content than any other generation of human beings before us, the words we read and voices we hear either nourish our souls or deplete our self-esteem. They can guide us toward growth or keep us stuck. They can open our hearts to vulnerability or shove us into shame.

Hitting the Follow button is a choice—a significant one at that. We must choose wisely.

Action Steps

In order to step forward into freedom and gain clarity on how to develop a healthier relationship with the barrage of external opinions, we need to take action and be aware of what our mind is consuming on a regular basis. I have developed a framework to help you identify the opinions that matter, audit existing influences in your environment, and cultivate a healthy space for personal development. Let's get to it.

Choose Your Inner Circle

First, think about the three people whose opinions matter most to you and assess why you hold their viewpoints in high regard. Feel free to create a longer list of names if you would like to dig deeper, but starting with three is sufficient as a jumping-off point.

Name	Why does this person's opinion matter to me?

Once you have completed this exercise, let's analyze your qualitative reasoning behind why you chose the names that you did. Do you see any similarities? What conclusions, both positive and negative, do you draw from this?

Knowing *why* someone's opinion matters to you is just as important as the people who you identify as key thought partners in your life. It illuminates how you are assigning value—and that is a clarifying tool for becoming more self-aware.

Be wary of placing too much importance on proximity (people who are physically closest to you) and longevity of the relationship (people who have been around you the longest amount of time). Neither of these factors are inherently a bad or good thing; it is just important to acknowledge that we may give more value to those qualities unknowingly.

Getting clarity about the criteria for whose input you

allow into your inner circle is imperative. Otherwise, one day you might discover that you evolved into who people thought you should be rather than blossoming into the best version of the person that you already are.

Diversify Your Feedback Portfolio

Just like with finances, you shouldn't throw all of your earnings into risky stock options or keep them stagnant in a low-interest savings account—you need to diversify your feedback portfolio.

If you have too much positive feedback, then you run the risk of an inflated ego with infinite blind spots. If you have too much negative feedback, then you run the risk of feeling discouraged or too fearful to take action.

If you look around at your sources of feedback and they all look the same, think the same, and fail to hold you accountable, that isn't a healthy sphere of influence—it is an echo chamber. As we have learned from neuroscience research, we are more likely to cultivate close relationships with people who think like we do. It can be tempting to cling to the comfortable rather than remain curious and open-minded; however, it is a challenge that I want you to take seriously.

Opinions that merely indulge your confirmation bias will nonetheless keep you precisely where you are with no opportunity for genuine growth. Repeating the same patterns of thinking and doing the same behaviors over and over again will never yield a different outcome.

It is important to strike a balance with people that you trust. You want to be simultaneously supported and safe, while being equally challenged and empowered to move beyond the familiar.

Here's one way to think about it:

- Positive or affirming feedback: Whose words make you feel the most encouraged, empowered, and inspired? Who are your biggest cheerleaders?
- Critical or growth feedback: Who do you trust to tell you the truth? Who will challenge you to grow in alignment with your values?
- Diversified feedback: Who has a different lived experience than you? Who brings a unique perspective or alternative viewpoint to the table?

Discern What to Take to Heart

When we share our lives with those around us, present our thoughts in the workplace, or live in accordance with our values, we are bound to get feedback on a one-to-one level. This is slightly different than our interactions that are further removed and often take place in a one-to-many format (social media being the most common example).

When making an assessment on whether to take someone's feedback to heart in closer proximity scenarios, ask yourself these five questions first:

- Is this individual someone who you respect or admire?
- Do they have knowledge or experience in this particular arena?
- Does this person accept you for who you *truly* are and have your best interests at heart?
- Do they understand who you aspire to become?
- Do they support your personal growth?

These questions are a helpful starting place to understand how to place value on comments, critiques, and even affirmation from external sources. As always, this list is not exhaustive, and someone falling short in one category does not disqualify what they have to say. Often times there is truth even in the feedback we disagree with. It is up to us to find it and determine if it is worth holding on to.

Audit Your Digital Feed

At least once a year, I recommend that you audit the existing digital channels of input in your life. Take a quick peek at the broad scope of content that you are consuming on a daily basis and ask yourself, Is this still serving me?

What accounts do you follow that

- Encourage you to live with bold, brave, and boundless courage;

- Inspire you to try new things and be your authentic self;
- Challenge you to grow, to learn, to think beyond the realm of your comfort zone;
- Cultivate a space of support and safety;
- Empower you to take action and make your impact on the world?

Additionally, think about what accounts leave you feeling the opposite of all of those aforementioned things. What content perhaps sways you to feel discouraged, keeps you stuck in limiting beliefs, doesn't align with your values or the person you are becoming?

After your audit, it is time to take action. Hit that Unfollow button. Find fresh sources of inspiration to follow. Engage with accounts that are in alignment with your vision, mission, and values. Remove yourself from groups that distract you from what matters most. Plug into communities that foster genuine belonging where you feel seen, heard, and valued.

Your social media feed should fuel you up like tiny gas stations on the long and winding road trip that is your life. When you pick up your phone, is something being added to your hypothetical tank or taken from it? This doesn't mean that you need to feel happy every time that you scroll. It does mean, however, that the content you are consuming should lead you closer toward the person that you desire to become rather than contributing negatively to your mental well-being.

And please remember...you are not always going to get it right.

There is no such thing as a perfect feed because there is no such thing as a perfect person, and it is human beings, after all, that get behind the keyboard. In the space past your sphere of authority and just at the farthest reaches of your sphere of influence lies the vast universe of things you cannot control.

If you have something to say, other people will have opinions. As we have established, that is a guarantee.

Remember that day I posted a picture of a fox and nearly brought my entire neighborhood to the brink of war for a very tense twenty-four-hour period? *Yeah, good times!*

There are going to be moments where even the spaces and people you intentionally bring into your life take you on emotional detours that you could not have anticipated. Learn from those moments, approach them with radical curiosity, and give yourself grace.

Remember: the thing about opinions is that they are everywhere, everybody has one, and they deeply influence us. We cannot control what other people think, but we can take action to control whose opinions we are allowing into our daily lives. We can be intentional with the sources of feedback that we trust. We can cultivate spaces that simultaneously allow us to nurture a positive view of ourselves and remain open to growth and improvement.

If you have been a passive bystander to the barrage of

opinions swirling around you, let this be a reminder that you have the power to take back control of the voices you allow to speak into your life. Small shifts in this arena can have a tremendous impact on how you feel about yourself and others. Take it one step at a time and watch it change your life.

CHAPTER 5

CRANK UP THE VOLUME

Sometimes the best way to find yourself is to lose sight of everyone else's expectations.

Sometimes that means grabbing the steering wheel away from the opinions of others, even the people closest to you, and yanking it hard in another direction.

I am talking tires skidding, smoke rising off the asphalt, and engine revving as you make a U-turn that sends that little hula girl on the dashboard shaking like Shakira's "Hips Don't Lie" and catapult yourself onto a dirt road that leads only God knows where.

There may come a time when you need to throw your foot

on the gas and accelerate like your life depends on it. Knowing when to speed off into the unknown or turn around and face the fears you have been running from requires you to hear and trust your inner voice.

It sounds so simple and yet it is common for us to become wrapped up in the thoughts of others—so much so that we have a hard time distinguishing our own authentic voice in the cacophony of opinions. It is also common for our inner voices to be clouded by soundtracks of doubt and insecurity that play on repeat as our confidence fades quietly into the background.

All of us struggle with this to some degree, so how do we go about nurturing our own inner voice and learning to trust it? How do we strengthen our self-esteem in a world that benefits so fully from our insecurities and doubts?

All of this brings me back to a conversation that I had a few years ago over lunch.

"Did you know that some people have an internal monologue?" my friend asked me one afternoon.

I stared at her with a puzzled expression as I popped another piece of sushi into my mouth.

"Wait—you don't? You seriously don't have an obnoxious little voice in your head?" I asked her.

Her jaw dropped open a bit and she looked at me with astonishment. "You are telling me that you are one of those people? You can hear yourself think? You can narrate your entire life in your mind?" she asked.

"Um, yes...You can't?" I responded. I genuinely thought

this was something that everyone could do. As it turns out, not everyone has an internal monologue.

The first time you learned about this I bet you were equally as astonished as I was. And if this is the very first time you are hearing this now, I will gladly give you a moment to pull up your phone and go down the informational rabbit hole. Circle back here when you are done, okay?

The truth is that my internal monologue is a real pain sometimes. I could sit here and pretend like I have perfected the art of positive self-talk, but I haven't. I often research and write about the very things that I struggle with most...and this is one of them. (*Which is perhaps why I felt that it deserved its very own chapter!*)

There are days where my own inner voice goes a little rogue.

On those days, she's like a DJ that likes to play the same tracks over and over again in painful succession. Trying to sleep in those moments is nearly impossible because my mind has the volume cranked up and the metaphorical music won't stop...it is like:

Welcome to your brain.

This evening's entertainment will be a prerecorded soundtrack called "What Are Other People Going to Think?" from an album that gets a lot of unintended airtime around here. This certainly isn't the first time you have heard it. The lyrics will likely sound familiar. They go like this:

What are other people going to think of me?

What if I fail? What if this is all just a big mistake?

What if I make a fool of myself in front of everyone?

What if they realize I am an imposter? If they think I am not good enough?

What if that person who judged me was right? What if I am a disappointment?

Will I let everyone down? Will I let myself down?

Even when you want to turn it off, this song has a tendency to consume all of your attention and stay stuck in your head for hours.

If you know all of the words, that is because this has been one of the most frequently played tracks in your mind for as long as you can remember. You might think it will fade out of popularity and disappear into irrelevance...However, just like Rick Astley's "Never Gonna Give You Up," it keeps coming back on over and over again, sucking a little more life out of you every time.

Okay, enough of that. I want to take a moment to pause right here and ask you for a giant favor. I want you to read through those questions again, removing the musical metaphors.

I want you to pause at each line, reading the words slowly and with intention.

I want you to think about the number of times that questions like those have stopped you from trying something new, sharing your heart, being your authentic self, or letting go of something or someone no longer meant for you. How many times have the opinions of others popped into your head before your own voice rose to the surface? How many times have you resorted to soaking those narratives up like a sponge and allowing them to live rent-free in your mind?

If you are anything like me, you do this far more times than you would care to admit. Just like I confessed earlier, this is something I have personally battled with for years.

Being the nerd that I am, this led me to research the ways in which we foster positive attitudes about ourselves and strengthen our underlying self-esteem. Let's break it down.

Self-Esteem Is the Key

"Self-esteem" is a term used in psychology to reflect a person's overall evaluation of their own worth. Simply put, it is the opinion that you hold of yourself.[1]

Self-esteem is made up of a collection of attributes, some of which include your self-image, your values and perceived success in living up to them, your accomplishments, and how other people perceive you. This foundational opinion is deeply connected to and influenced by how you accept, respect, and believe in yourself. The more positive the overall

---

1. Courtney Ackerman, "What Is Self-Esteem? A Psychologist Explains," PositivePsychology.com, May 23, 2018, https://positivepsychology.com/self-esteem/.

perception of these qualities and characteristics is, the higher your self-esteem becomes.[2]

How does this play out behaviorally? When someone has high self-esteem, they are likely to share their opinion, stand up for themselves and others, communicate their needs, and feel they are worthy of the good things in their life. On the other hand, when someone has low self-esteem, they are more likely to be people-pleasing, diminish the value of their own opinion, feel they are never good enough, avoid taking risks, struggle to say no, compare themselves to others, and view themselves as inferior.

One of my favorite ways to think about self-esteem is through an equation developed by renowned American philosopher and psychologist William James over a century ago. He defined it as "the ratio of our actualities to our supposed potentialities."[3]

In the traditional definition, he used the terms "actualities" and "potentialities"—however, for the sake of modernizing this equation, let's think about pretensions as our aspirations. These are the hopes and dreams that make up the possibility of what could be.[4] This simple equation transformed my understanding of the concept.

2. *APA Dictionary of Psychology*, s.v. "self-esteem (*n.*)," accessed October 31, 2022, https://dictionary.apa.org/self-esteem.

3. William James, *The Principles of Psychology* (Cambridge, MA: Harvard University Press, 1983; first published in 1890).

4. Christopher J. Mruk, "The Crucial Issue of Defining Self Esteem," chap. 1 in *Self-Esteem and Positive Psychology: Research, Theory, and Practice*, 4th ed. (New York: Springer, 2013).

$$Self\text{-}esteem = \frac{Success}{Aspirations}$$

This is powerful for a whole host of reasons. First, it points out that our self-esteem is dynamic and can be changed. Similarly, it reminds us that how we interpret our own reality against the backdrop of what could be is within our control. This gives us the ability to tinker with the numerator and denominator to shift our self-esteem in a more positive direction.

Think of it like this:

Someone can be incredibly successful and still have low self-esteem. Perhaps it is because they hold themselves to an unrealistic standard or aspire to an unattainable reality and therefore the denominator becomes incredibly large. Perhaps it is because they are measuring themselves against the wrong aspirations entirely—like chasing someone else's definition of success rather than their own. This means that their success pales in comparison to the inappropriately high denominator, and they struggle with their worth as a result.

On the flip side, someone could easily underestimate the numerator by not valuing their own success as well. They could dismiss their own accomplishments or talents, belittling the perspective of how valuable their unique giftings are. How we internally quantify our success matters to our overall perception of self.

There is a famous quote attributed to Albert Einstein that says,

> Everybody is a genius. But if you judge a fish by its ability to climb a tree, it will live its whole life believing that it is stupid.

Whether it was in fact Einstein who said those words or not is up for debate; however, the concept is absolutely critical to how we measure success for ourselves and others.

If you line up every animal in the entire animal kingdom—the mammals, fish, birds, reptiles, and amphibians—and determine their worth by their ability to climb a tree, you are going to miss the unique strengths that each of them possesses. You will tell the fish they can't cut it and the birds that they are cheating when they swoop into the sky without touching the trunk at all.

We see this in office settings all the time. Someone may be a math wizard or crush operationalizing a business by being an effective integrator, whereas another person is a creative genius who develops new ideas and solves unique problems by thinking outside the box. Both have a dramatic effect on the company's success.

However, if a company only values worth in terms of a single success measurement rather than adopting a more dynamic approach to gauging performance, they risk losing incredible talent and building homogenous teams that fail in the long run.

How many of us are like fish looking up at the tree and comparing ourselves to the animals who find it easy to climb? How many of us don't recognize that if we were instead measuring ourselves against our ability to swim, we would have a vastly different perception of self?

Defining success on your own terms based on your own unique giftings and talents is important. This is a reason why at the end of the day, other people are neither your competition nor are they an accurate representation of how you "measure up." Your success will look different from everyone else's. There is so much freedom in that.

I also love the self-esteem equation for one more reason. You are allowed to have weaknesses that don't detract from your worth. You get to curate which considerations go into the equation altogether.

If you don't desire to be fluent in Lithuanian, then you won't feel like a failure for not knowing the language. If you don't aspire to be a professional ice-skater, then your ability to do elaborate spins on the ice won't be the make-or-break metric to determine your worth.

How you define success and what component pieces go into it matter.

You don't have to be good at everything, and being inherently bad at one thing doesn't mean that you are bad overall. This is a simple and yet powerful construct. You craft your own determination of what matters. That is for you and you alone to decide.

When you realize that milestones and finish lines and measuring posts are arbitrary, the next phase of your life begins. You have the power to choose what success looks like.

Gutsy guiding activities and questions:

- Make a list of the five accomplishments that you are most proud of. What are they? Why do they matter so much to you and what do they say about you?
- What are attributes of yourself that you admire or view positively?
- Ask three people who know you best to share a few things that they love about you and/or think you are excellent at. Compare those insights to the ones that you hold of yourself. What are the similarities? What attributes do you need to add to your list that were missing before the exercise?

Confront Negative Thinking Patterns

When you find yourself in patterns of negative thinking, it is important to remember that there are alternative ways to view any given situation. Your first take isn't always the best one. Heck, your first take might not even be accurate.

Pay attention to negative thought patterns that may be wearing down your self-esteem, especially those that aren't rooted in reality. These can include the following:

- **All-or-nothing thinking.** This type of thinking involves only viewing situations in extremes, often in a black-or-white manner. Something is either all good or all bad, either a success or a total failure. It leaves no room for shades of gray or room for eventual improvement. It takes "I failed at one task" and turns it into "I fail at everything."
- **Mistaking feelings for facts.** Our reality feels true to us, but that doesn't necessarily mean that it is, in fact, the truth. Sometimes we confuse how we feel with how things realistically are. It can take a bump in the road and turn it into a larger piece of our identity. For example, "Since I feel like a failure, then I must be a failure."
- **Mental filtering.** This occurs when you filter out the positive and focus only on the negative. This type of thinking can dramatically distort your perception of a person, a situation, or even yourself. It is like when someone gets ten great reviews or comments on something and then one negative one. Mental filtering, in this case, might mean excluding all the positive sentiments and dwelling only on the negative.[5]

---

5. "Self-Esteem: Take Steps to Feel Better about Yourself," Mayo Clinic, July 6, 2022, https://www.mayoclinic.org/healthy-lifestyle/adult-health/in-depth/self-esteem /art-20045374.

We all have negative thoughts from time to time. Catching these patterns and developing techniques to bolster our self-esteem despite them are the key.

Turning Up the Volume on Positive Self-Talk

The key to drowning out the cacophony of negativity—either from external forces or internal narratives—is to replace it with something stronger. Since I am on a musical metaphor kick in this chapter, you can think of it a little like this:

Grab a self-love speaker in the form of your inner voice and crank up the volume. Let a new sound fill the static, a fresh perspective blast through the room. Turn up the bass and let it become a roaring freight train of confidence until the ground rumbles beneath your feet.

This requires more than shouting positive affirmations at yourself in the mirror. While I am a big fan of speaking positively to yourself and I am not here to diminish the power of that practice by any means, I have seen how quickly this concept has become watered down, and I fear that it becomes less effective as a result.

If the only thing you do to combat negative self-talk is to tell yourself, "You are amazing!" every single day, you are missing a genuine opportunity to move the needle farther. A small amount of additional intentionality can make your affirmations even more powerful. Here are some examples of ways to do precisely that.

1. Identify Situations That Affect Your Self-Esteem

When do you find yourself inundated with negative self-talk? What circumstances ignite those insecurities? Create a short list of these situations and bring them to your attention. Identify any trends you see (crisis, conflict, and change are often big ones) to help guide when and where to leverage the power of affirmations proactively.

Also, look for people who impact your self-esteem either positively or negatively and explore why you believe that might be the case. Do you tend to find yourself feeling a particular way repeatedly after spending time with someone? Don't ignore that feeling.

2. Be Immediate, Consistent, and Repetitive

When you catch yourself in a spiral of negative self-talk, do not repress or resist acknowledging the situation. Accept how you feel and develop a consistent practice of addressing it in the moment. Try asking yourself, Are these beliefs true or based on false ideas?

If the negative beliefs are false, replace them with truth and use that as an affirmation going forward. Flip the script in the moment, speak the positive affirmation over yourself, and make a mental note to strengthen that area later by doing some repetitions. Think of it like affirmation weight lifting. Repetition builds habit and helps to rewire the brain. Or you can think of it like depositing a dollar into the self-esteem bank account every time you intentionally affirm the very thing you were struggling with.

If there is underlying truth to your negative self-talk, then ask yourself, How would I say this to a friend? Adjust how you communicate with yourself and reframe your language to be kinder and even empowering. This leans on the power of self-awareness and allows you to acknowledge your imperfections through a more accepting frame of mind. One trick I personally use is to turn my imperfections or insecurities into superpowers.

For example, if you're going into an event and catch yourself in a negative self-talk spiral thinking, "I am awkward and no one is going to like me," try flipping it into something earnest yet affirming like, "My quirkiness is precisely what sets me apart and makes me a blast to be around," or perhaps something like, "My awkwardness is relatable, and people love that I have the courage to truly be myself."

When you accept the very things that you used to fear would make you unlovable or unworthy and you flip those traits into being your internalized superpower, something profound happens. You stop allowing those insecurities to hold you back, and you move forward with a more accepting perception of yourself.

3. Make Sure Your Affirmations Are Serving You

Sometimes people affirm themselves for things they aren't even struggling with by adopting someone else's list of affirmations. In other words, don't just say affirmations for the heck of it. Be intentional about the phrases that you choose.

Where do you need to shift your mindset the most? Target your needs rather than reciting phrases just for the heck of it. When you proactively align your affirmations with the things that you genuinely are struggling with, it will have a more positive impact.

Here are some quick tips for making affirmations actionable:

- Once you identify the self-talk phrases that have the most impact for you, create a habit of saying them every day. Pin them to your bulletin board. Make them the background on your phone. Recite them every morning like schoolkids say the Pledge of Allegiance. Record yourself saying your affirmations and play it through your headphones like a podcast when you need an extra dose of positive thinking.

- Proactively include affirmations in your schedule, especially in advance of situations that have a tendency to negatively impact your self-esteem. Think of this like putting sunscreen on before going to the beach. You don't wait until after your skin burns to apply it. You lather up before going outside.

- When you speak to yourself, you are also speaking to that smaller self within. Remember that. Envision that. Pin a photo of yourself as a child to your bulletin board or make it the background of your phone if it helps to shift your internal soundtrack toward a kinder, more empathetic version of you.

- Get an accountability partner or turn this into a family activity. Craft affirmations with someone that you trust, or help your kids create their own affirmations and practice saying them together. You can even make a family affirmation manifesto and post it on the refrigerator to say every morning before walking out the door. Bringing others into this practice can strengthen it and widen its impact.

My challenge to you is to love yourself fiercely. To speak words of affirmation and acknowledgment into the wounds of your heart that need healing.

There will always be someone out there who, in their own pain, fails to recognize the incredible gift that you are to this world...Please don't allow that person to be you.

Don't let the negativity win. Don't let the opinions of others hold more value than your opinion of yourself. Don't let the voices that surround you drown out the voice from within you.

When you are tempted to tear yourself down, imagine saying those words to a much younger you. I want you to see the face of your smaller self looking back at you in the mirror. I want you to imagine that tiny smile so full of hope and those eyes so full of wonder.

Be their cheerleader. Be their advocate. Be their champion

in a world that is set on seeing them struggle with insecurity, doubt, and fear.

Rise up and be the positive voice that you have always needed to hear within. Crank up the volume. Put the positive self-talk soundtracks on repeat. Watch it change your world.

CHAPTER 6

CENTER OF ATTENTION

I grew up going to Catholic school, which meant that I wore a uniform every day from kindergarten to twelfth grade.

I was never particularly a fan of those uniforms—a white button-down shirt always tucked into a skirt that, due to my height, was always deemed just a little too short.

Teachers took the dress code almost as seriously as they took the Bible, and there was a ridiculous amount of pressure placed upon us to look a certain way.

I remember that as I got older, I began to feel so self-conscious about my body. I was always taller than other girls and a bit curvier. All of that attention placed on how we needed to look caused me so much anxiety about getting in trouble or being perceived as unworthy for things I couldn't control.

My legs grew longer, and so my skirts became shorter. My curvy build meant that I wore a bigger size than most of my friends. My boobs just appeared one day, and that meant leaving the second button of my shirt unbuttoned felt slightly more scandalous than it ever had before.

Some of you might think I am overreacting...and yet there are others who have felt that familiar pang of shame in their gut when they too were called out in front of the entire class for a uniform violation.

Mortifying. Embarrassing. Shameful.

I still feel uneasy remembering what it was like to have the figurative spotlight shined on me, the teacher calling me over, making me reach down my arms to see if the hem of my skirt met my fingertips or not. Other kids watched. Some laughed.

I was called out and ridiculed in front of everyone. I was already insecure about how I looked, and it felt like I was being picked apart for missing a few centimeters of fabric.

It wasn't until adulthood that I truly started to unpack the deeply rooted feelings of shame that I had carried with me from that single uniform requirement. It was such a tiny thing, and yet...it ignited an insecurity deep within me that never went away.

I had come to inaccurately believe that my worth and value were tied to other people's approval over my appearance. I began to value the way things looked more than value the way they actually were. I felt uncomfortable existing in my own body because I felt like I was under a microscope—as if everyone were scrutinizing me the same way that teacher did.

By the time I made it to high school, my mom had started to notice how much this affected me. I remember getting ready for homecoming my freshman year and not even wanting to go to the dance. I tugged at my dress. I couldn't decide on a pair of shoes. I judged myself so harshly in the mirror.

My mom saw me getting worked up shortly before it was time to go and asked me what was bothering me. "Do I look okay?" I asked. "I am worried about what other people are going to think about how I look. My dress, my hair, everything—I am just not sure if it is good enough."

The thing that my mom said next has stuck with me for the rest of my life.

Looking at me, she responded, "They aren't going to be thinking about what you look like at all. Not one bit. I am willing to bet that they are more worried about how they look and what other people are thinking of them."

Ugh. That was when it hit me.

Other people do not care as much about you as you think they do.

The Spotlight Effect

Trust me—they do not pay as much attention to you as you may believe. They don't spend hours picking apart the things you said or criticizing the way you looked. They aren't up late at night, running through all of the interactions that you had together analyzing your behavior. I am willing to bet they don't give you much thought at all.

That sounds incredibly harsh, and it truly isn't meant to be. I don't say that to be hurtful or flippant or unkind. It is simply the truth. Human beings are incredibly self-interested.

Other people aren't spending all of their time worrying about you, because they are far more concerned with themselves. They are likely navigating those same limiting beliefs and insecurities themselves. There is a far better chance they are worrying about what you think than investing their time passing judgment.

No one judges your every decision or remembers your every mistake. The people who you think are scrutinizing you are likely too busy worrying about what other people think about them—in the same way that you worry about the opinions other people hold of you.

Oh, and frankly, if there is a particular person who spends all of their time picking you apart and throwing criticism your way, that says more about their inner turmoil than it does about your character. That isn't an indication that you are doing anything wrong. That is the sign of someone who is hurting themselves and truly needs help.

Research provides evidence to support the belief that people significantly overestimate how much attention other people are paying to them. Psychologists have dubbed this phenomenon the spotlight effect.

The spotlight effect occurs when a person becomes overly self-conscious and tends to believe that there is a figurative spotlight on them at all times. It feels as if this spotlight highlights all of our imperfections, mistakes, and flaws.

This is a type of cognitive distortion known as an egocentric bias. This bias misrepresents the way we see the world by leading us to rely too heavily on our own perspective. We effectively center ourselves rather than adjusting to take other viewpoints into account.[1]

On the one hand, it is a tough pill to swallow: no one cares about you as much as you think they do. On the other hand, it is incredibly liberating, isn't it? No one will ever care as much about your flaws as you do. Very few people will even take note of your mistakes at all.

In 2000, Tom Gilovich and colleagues ran a series of studies on the spotlight effect and published their findings in the *Journal of Personality and Social Psychology.* In one study, the researchers gathered groups of students to complete an unrelated task and randomly assigned one of the students in each group to wear an embarrassing shirt. The students wearing the shirt severely overestimated how many of their peers would take note of what they were wearing.

They predicted 50 percent would notice the ridiculous attire; however, only 25 percent could recall what was on the shirt. These numbers shifted significantly in a second study where

1. "Why Do We Feel Like We Stand Out More Than We Really Do? The Spotlight Effect, Explained," The Decision Lab, accessed November 1, 2022, https://thedecisionlab.com /biases/spotlight-effect.

the embarrassing shirt was swapped out for a standard shirt of a recognizable figure—Bob Marley, Jerry Seinfeld, or Martin Luther King Jr. Again the students wearing the shirt assumed 50 percent of their peers would be able to recall what they were wearing, but only 10 percent of students could accurately identify the correct figure.[2]

Think about that last number—10 percent.

That is such a small percentage of people that could immediately recall the shirt design. Imagine how that number probably dropped in the days, weeks, and months after the interaction. Did anyone even remember at all a month later? How about a year later?

Everyone is the protagonist of their own story. The world doesn't revolve around any single one of us, and yet sometimes we lose sight of that. In the realm of combatting the fear of what other people think, remember that other people simply aren't focusing on you nearly as much as you think they are. Other people are likely too busy worrying about themselves.

Memories Fade

Now that we have determined that people have a tendency to overestimate how much other people are thinking about them, we need to put our own hesitations into perspective.

---

2. Thomas Gilovich, Victoria Husted Medvec, and Kenneth Savitsky, "The Spotlight Effect in Social Judgment: An Egocentric Bias in Estimates of the Salience of One's Own Actions and Appearance," *Journal of Personality and Social Psychology* 78, no. 2 (2000): 211–222.

Just because something is deeply embarrassing to us and therefore is seared into our memory—like the day I was called up to the front of the class for a uniform violation—does not mean that it carries the same amount of emotional weight to other people.

I guarantee you that the teacher who called me out in front of the class wouldn't even remember my name today...I was perhaps the only one in that entire room who still remembers what happened. When our emotions are heightened around a situation, our memories can take on greater meaning to us than to other people.

We have a tendency to magnify situations in our mind in which we made mistakes, failed, were publicly criticized, or were embarrassed in front of others—without realizing that this perspective is not shared to that same extent with others.

I have managed a lot of Facebook groups, some of which are highly active, with tens of thousands of people interacting on any given day. I cannot even begin to tell you the number of times over the years that people have come after me in direct messages, disagreeing with something that I did or said. Especially when it came to our rules and guidelines that prevented things like self-promotion or determined how long it occasionally took for posts to get approved—I have been on the receiving end of some vitriolic dialogue.

Reading what people posted on some of these threads, you would think that I had murdered their cat when a post was delayed moving through approval because it was a holiday weekend. I kid you not.

Early on, it really used to affect me. I have a very soft heart, and getting yelled at in all caps either publicly or in a direct message made my stomach turn. Here's the thing: I remember the people who were cruel to me—especially the ones who went above and beyond to tear me apart. I remember their profile pictures, the words they said—absolutely everything. Our brains do a good job marking down moments of pain and shame to ensure we avoid them in the future.

However, the people who wrote those comments to me... well, most of them have little to no recollection. That is the strangest thing of all.

I have met some of these people in person, and they are unbelievably kind to me in real life—most had completely forgotten how they'd reacted to me on the internet several years before. It even gets a little awkward when someone responds positively to a recent piece of content that I have shared only to see how they spoke to me in the past as it pops up in the feed. You would be amazed by how many apologies I have received five to six years later for someone's past frustration over a post not getting published fast enough or a question around why something was removed for violating a guideline.

I may carry the pain of that experience with me...but they forget it as quickly as it happened. I am not saying that makes it right; however, it has become blatantly clear to me that other people simply do not remember most of their past interactions with you. The very things that are seared into my memory were not even worth holding on to for them.

Our attention is fleeting. Our memories are quick to fade.

All of this to say, when your fears around what others might think of you if you fail hold you back from moving forward, remember that there is a good chance that very few people are even going to care. There is an even greater chance that virtually no one will remember your mishap long into the future.

Our own inflated sense of importance means that we believe our mistakes matter far more to other people than they in fact do. There is a shelf life on the length of time that we hold on to other people's failings.

We only have so much shelf space up there in our brain, and holding on to every time that every person we have ever interacted with made a mistake or didn't succeed—well, it just isn't our top priority. When you start to step out of your comfort zone and beyond the shadows that you thought were keeping you safe, you will start to realize that the same people you were afraid would judge you are too busy judging themselves.

Consider asking yourself these questions:

- What would your life be like if you believed that no one would ever take note of your mistakes? What choices would you have made differently?
- Is there a memory from your past that you have been holding on to that can now be understood in a different way? Consider implementing what you

have learned by rewriting this particular narrative through the lens of your older self.

- How might your future look if you remind yourself just how little attention people give to your mishaps and failures? How can you experience that freedom in your choices?

- How can you be better about giving yourself the grace you deserve when you make mistakes? How can you foster a more nurturing and forgiving inner voice?

There is something deeply freeing about realizing that you are not, in fact, under a spotlight or being observed under a microscope.

Even for those who live very public lives and invite perhaps more scrutiny than the average person, the attention span of the public eye is very short. What everyone was fired up about one day will be collecting cobwebs in collective memories the next.

You don't have to remain frozen in fear. You can get out there and make mistakes. You may just be surprised by how much more free you feel when you remind yourself how little people are taking notice of your flaws in the first place.

CHAPTER 7

DECISIONS, DECISIONS

Several years ago, I was offered a book deal.

I was not a writer at the time…or perhaps I should say that my writing was limited to long captions on Instagram and the occasional blog post. The offer came out of the blue and was completely unexpected.

I received an email from a big-name publisher explaining that one of their acquisitions editors had been following me on social media, watching my small-business advocacy from afar, and recommended me as a potential new author.

I had always dreamt of writing a book. This was the dream that I had carried with me from my days as the editor of my high school newspaper. Becoming a writer was that moonshot career path that I always hoped I would have the chance to pursue, but it hadn't materialized.

However, there was one problem with this otherwise perfect opportunity: the publisher had a very clear vision for the book that they wanted to print, and it was up to me to decide if I would be the one to write it.

In earnest, the book concept wasn't what I had hoped it would be. That's not to say it was bad—it wasn't. Honestly, it was a great book idea. I just couldn't picture myself being the one to write it.

I was at war with myself from the moment I read through the contract. It was as if my head were screaming, "Take this offer, for goodness' sake—this is a sure thing. Who cares if it isn't the book that you want to write deep down? Bird in the hand and all that. Something is better than nothing!"

However, my equally passionate heart was shouting back, "You know that this isn't meant for you—go after what you truly want. Write the book that you have always wanted to write. Bet on yourself even if it means no future deals come. You can self-publish!"

Being pursued by a publisher out of the blue was a form of flattery that I had never experienced before. They offered me a book deal, for crying out loud…And I knew that if I turned them down, they would move on to the next person on their list. I was the replaceable one in this scenario.

I kept opening the email, reading the contract, marking it as unread, and continuing to procrastinate my decision. I felt like a complete idiot for even questioning it, but I continued dragging my feet nonetheless.

That's when an author friend, Jon Acuff, introduced me to his literary agents and asked them if they would be open to advising me on next steps. They agreed to hop on a quick call as a favor to Jon, and I was open with them about everything. I rambled on and on about the pros and cons, when one of them finally stopped me politely and asked, "Is this the book that you have always wanted to write?"

I shook my head no. It wasn't.

"If you say no to this offer and write the book you have in your heart, knowing that there is a chance no publisher may be interested in it down the line, would you be okay with that?"

When the question was framed that way, the answer was easy.

"Of course; I would be okay with that. I would self-publish," I responded.

"Then I think you have your answer. Turn them down, work on writing the book you are meant to write, and bet on yourself."

That little nod of permission, that gentle nudge to go after what I truly wanted, was enough for me to turn down the big-name publisher.

I declined the offer, and the next day I began outlining what would become my first book. I poured my heart and soul into that manuscript. I knew that it was a book worth fighting for...and so I did.

Sometimes failing in the pursuit of what you really want is still better than never having tried at all. Either way, you'll never know until you lift your feet from the comfortable steadiness of the ground and choose a direction for yourself.

Backseat Drivers

This entire chapter is about discernment. When should you say yes, and when should you say no? What opportunities should you take, and which should you turn down? When is it time to keep fighting for what you want, and when is letting go in fact the braver, better choice?

Everyone will have something to say about it, but you call the shots. You are the only person who is living your life. Many opinions are worth taking into consideration; however, there will come a time when you need to decide.

And isn't choosing often the hardest part?

I have always found it to be the case that indecision goes hand in hand with the fear of judgment, the fear of criticism, and living for the approval of others. It is that momentary pause, that pattern of second-guessing, that inhibits you from taking definitive action and feeling confident in your own choices.

Because, as we have established, everyone is going to have

an opinion about the decisions that you make. From your closest family and friends to your mentor to the motivational voices on social media…Heck, even I would likely have something to say if you asked me.

Human beings will always have a point of view, a comment to add, a suggestion or different approach they would encourage you to take. That's not inherently the problem.

The indecisiveness that arises when we allow that multitude of voices to become louder than our own internal voice is the real threat. When we surrender the direction of our lives over to a massive group of people with conflicting interests and ideas of where we should go, we are more likely than not to remain stuck in place.

It would be like driving a car without a map where every passenger is shouting for you to go in a different direction. *Turn left! Turn right! Stop! Speed up!* I don't know about you, but I can't handle even one backseat driver when I am behind the wheel…It makes me a flustered, frustrated, and confused mess of a person.

So, when we find ourselves struggling to uncover what it is that we truly want, how do we pick the best path forward? That's precisely what this chapter is about.

When Should You Say Yes?

I was at a conference several years ago when a keynote speaker rallied the crowd by having them chant, "If it is not a hell yes, then it is a no!" Back and forth they went, and the audience was eating it up. There was clapping and cheering.

As much as I loved the enthusiasm, I couldn't help but shift uncomfortably in my seat. I disagreed with parts of that phrase. I hated that advice.

Okay, I can hear my mom in my head now saying, *Whoa, now! Natalie, "hate" is a very strong word!*—so, perhaps let me correct myself before diving into a personal hot take.

I strongly dislike this advice...because most of the time, for most people, in most seasons of life, this advice falls flat. Does that cover it? I am winking with a hint of sarcasm in my voice because I have a slight bone to pick with advice like this.

If it is not a hell yes, then it is a no!

The saying sounds good, though, doesn't it? I know that it does. It sounds freaking fantastic.

Only do the things that fire you up. Don't waste your time on people or opportunities that aren't bringing you joy. If you aren't enthusiastic about something, don't go after it.

I am a big proponent of knowing when to say no and using that word early and often...Genuinely, I really am. I even have a sticky note next to my computer that says, "No is a full sentence." I am at a stage in my life where I have the privilege of saying no. But it wasn't always this way. It isn't this way for a lot of people.

My professional success is due in part to all of the opportunities I took that were far from a "hell yes." I did a lot of things that so many coaches and educators tell you not to do as a small-business owner…and yet, by trusting myself to make the best decisions for my business, I opened a lot of doors that never would have been available to me otherwise.

What about all the opportunities that are a far cry from a "hell yes" but that will put you on the path to being able to be more selective one day? Sometimes saying yes to what would otherwise be a "hell no" leads you toward the life that you want. It takes guts to put in the earnest work required to make your dreams happen.

When I first started my photography business, I was a full-time college student on financial aid with zero experience and no portfolio. My single mom had sacrificed a lot so that I could continue my education, and I wanted to prove to her that those sacrifices were worth it…that I wouldn't squander everything that she had worked so hard to give me.

My photography business was the way that I filled the gaps between my student loans and financial aid. It is how I paid for school and everything else. At the time, I didn't get to be choosy about who and what I photographed. I took whatever jobs I could get, and that meant that although I dreamt of being a wedding photographer, you could hire me to capture just about anything.

Five years later, when I had established my business and earned rave recommendations from past clients, I was in a vastly different place. I had more freedom to take creative risks and pursue personal projects just for fun. I could say no to opportunities that weren't in alignment with my larger vision because I had an abundance of inquiries coming in week to week.

At that stage of life, I was operating from a place of "If it isn't a hell yes, then it is a no." However, it took years of turning my less-than-hell-yes opportunities into stepping stones before I reached a point where I was able to be more selective about what I said yes to.

I am not trying to pick on this particular bit of advice. Frankly, it is one quote in a sea of sound bites and motivational speeches that directly ignore the varying positions of privilege or considerations that might make saying yes or no to certain opportunities easier for some people than for others. This just so happens to be the one that stands out the most in retrospect.

On the flip side, there will always be someone out there telling you to "say yes to all the things that scare you" or "leap and it will always work out in the end" without addressing the very real consequences of failure, overcommitment, or burnout. There are certainly two sides to this coin, and I have no interest in choosing one in this self-help standoff.

So, how do you discern when to say yes?

Here are some of the questions that I encourage you to take into consideration when choosing to agree to an opportunity or take on a new project. These questions are a good jumping-off point to help you create a framework of your own for making more intentional decisions.

You can steal my questions or write new ones. You can even consider creating a point scale to quantify opportunities as they arise (adding points for benefits, detracting for cost, and so on).

For those who struggle with indecision, the most important thing to do is to develop a repeatable and consistent system to serve as the foundation for your discernment process. In other words, you start by asking yourself how you feel about saying yes or no before looking externally for feedback. This is where developing a discernment process comes into play.

Here is a very simple framework for discerning when to say yes and when to say no.

Natalie's Should-I-Say-Yes Framework

1. Am I able to say yes to this opportunity given my current circumstances, resources, and prior commitments? (Or more simply put: Is it doable? Is it smart?)
   a. If you answer yes, continue forward.
   b. If you answer no, stop here. You must turn down the opportunity.
2. Do I want to say yes?
   a. If you answer yes, continue forward.

    b. If you answer no, pause and give this opportunity more intense scrutiny. Ask yourself, Is the cost of saying no to this something that I can live with? What is the benefit of saying yes and does that outweigh my lack of desire to do the work to get there? In other words, evaluate whether turning down this opportunity is something that you are able to do in this current season of your life before proceeding. Discern whether to move forward or stop here based on your response.

3. What is the cost of a yes? What will I have to give up if I agree to do this?

    a. Are you willing to pay that cost? If yes, continue forward.

    b. If no, stop here.

4. What are the time constraints?

    a. Are you able to allocate the time needed to take on this opportunity? If yes, this sounds like a winner.

    b. If no, consider if there is a way to delegate aspects of the opportunity elsewhere to make the time needed feasible. If you can outsource elements of the process or scale down the overall scope to meet existing commitments and constraints, go for it. If not, honor your time and let the opportunity pass.

Your decision-making framework should point you in the right direction of a decision and increase the likelihood of the best possible outcome. That way incorporating other people's guidance, suggestions, or opinions comes after you have checked in with your own intuition.

When you land on a decision, either a yes or a no, remember this: There is no right answer. There is only the best answer for you.

When Is It Time to Let Go?

That's the hard thing about hard things—there is no formula for dealing with them.
—BEN HOROWITZ

Making the decision to let go often terrifies even the bravest among us.

Perhaps it is admitting that our prior plan or path didn't work out. Perhaps it is realizing that a season in our lives is coming to an end or that something we thought would be everlasting turns out to be fleeting and temporary. Perhaps it is the judgment, criticism, gossip, or endless questions that come with unexpected changes. Perhaps it is the fear of the unknown—the uncertainty of what waits in the foggy future of something new.

Regardless of the reason, letting go or changing course is unsettling. You are not alone if you fear it. You are also not alone if that fear keeps you clinging to a career, a relationship, an opportunity, or a lifestyle that is no longer meant for you.

A bird in the hand is better than two in the bush—right? If you release the thing you have to pursue something better, you may fail somewhere along the way and be left empty-handed.

We have a tendency to settle for what is certain even when it isn't what is right for us. I truly believe that God Himself could try to pry our unhappiness, our broken relationships, our toxic jobs from our clenched fists to give us something better, and we would fight Him endlessly to cling to them.

We often choose the misery we know rather than the joy that could await us because there is a false sense of safety in the familiar.

However, the contrary can also be true. We are dynamic beings, and occasionally we have to navigate the "yes and" of life's complexities.

Sometimes choosing to hold on is the brave and necessary choice. Sometimes choosing to believe that things will get better, choosing to cling to hope that good things await you on the other side of this difficult season is the ultimate test of courage. Sometimes the gutsy choice is the choice to stay and fight for your first dream, rather than pivot to what could be next for you.

I cannot tell you when to hold on or when to let go—only

you can do that. So how do you decide? How do you discern whether you are moving forward in hope or holding back in fear?

After three failed rounds of fertility treatment while trying to conceive our second child, I was ready to throw in the towel. I was tired of trying so hard to have another baby, tired of the repeated disappointment, tired of the injections, doctor's visits, and pain. I was tired of seeing the look in my husband's eyes when all of that effort was for nothing.

I wasn't sure that I wanted to keep going and pursue a more intense course of action...so I took a few months off from treatment and gave my heart time to heal. When it came time to decide whether we were going forward with IVF, I vividly remember asking myself this question:

If I fail, is this something I can live with?

If I go through all of this again only for it to end in painful disappointment, will I truly be okay? Perhaps not right away, of course, but will I survive it?

There have been hundreds of thousands of others who have stood at the edge of that very same question with varying considerations.

For many, continuing onward with treatment meant a financial hardship that they were not able to risk. For others, the pain of enduring even more loss was not something that they could survive. There are an infinite number of considerations and equally as many hard choices that we are making every single day.

All paths forward are valid. To stop, to continue onward, to seek an alternative road—there isn't a single right choice. There is only a right choice for *you*.

We chose to move forward with IVF, and my daughter is the result of that cycle. She was our only day-five blastocyst. We transferred that little embryo, and by God's grace, several months later I was holding my baby girl, Harlow.

I am grateful that the fourth time turned out to be a success, but that isn't the takeaway here.

We live in a world where choosing to persevere is encouraged above all else. We live in a culture that tells us to try, try, try again until we succeed without addressing the very real trauma and consequences that often accompany that decision.

Although I chose to try once again, I did so knowing that I could handle the emotional, physical, and financial fallout if that attempt failed. I did so from a position of immense privilege. I did so with the support of my partner, my therapist, and a community that I knew could help me navigate the devastation that might await me on the other side.

That, as uncomfortable as it may be, is actually the point.

When making difficult decisions, we must be honest with ourselves about what failure would mean for us. Contrary to most of the popular self-help ideology out there, simply choosing to "imagine what could go right" and ignoring the very real consequences of "what could go wrong" isn't healthy.

It makes a great second step, a follow-up to what I am suggesting here, but it cannot be the only approach to analyzing the potential outcomes that sit before us.

We make better decisions when we are honest with ourselves about what we can and cannot handle. We make smarter choices when we have the courage to confront potential failure head-on and view it not through a lens of fear, but a perspective of hope.

Remember that courage doesn't always look like persevering. Sometimes courage means letting go of the life you thought you would have and being brave enough to face what awaits you on the other side of that decision.

It is okay not to take a risk when the resulting failure would have ruined you. That doesn't make you a coward. It means you can discern what you are willing to lose and what you aren't.

Sometimes the bravest thing we can do as human beings is to make a hard choice that we wish we never had to make. Sometimes the most courageous thing is simply to take action at all. When both roads ahead are difficult, moving forward regardless of direction requires us to rise above the false safety of stagnation.

The next time you hit a crossroads and you are struggling to choose whether to hold on or let go, whether to fight forward or surrender, ask yourself this hard but honest question:

If I fail, is that something I can live with?

When thinking through the question, I also recommend doing the following:

- Zoom in, not out. When making hard decisions, focus on the next step forward rather than running through the thousands of additional scenarios that could follow. Simplify as much as you can by concentrating on each sequential decision as it arises.
- Be honest with yourself. Don't sugarcoat the worst-case scenario. Don't catastrophize it either. What does failing honestly mean? What would that scenario look like? If you have a tendency to minimize or maximize negative outcomes, work with a trusted partner or professional to walk through these scenarios.
- Operate from a lens of hope rather than fear. When dealing with the potential for a negative outcome, fear has a tendency to creep in. Remind yourself that this is hypothetical and visualize an imaginary distance between you and the outcome. Then ask the question again.

Once you make your decision, also ask yourself these follow-up questions:

What will I need to get through the path that I have chosen? What people and resources must I have in place in order to move forward?

For me personally, this meant meeting weekly with a therapist throughout all of my fertility treatment and subsequent high-risk pregnancy. It meant confiding in those closest to me about my plans and engaging in support groups online with others who were going through similar situations. Take time to find a plan that works for you, and don't be afraid to get professional help or lean into a caring community.

Remember that you are never alone. Not in your successes and certainly not in your failures. We need one another in the same way that we need oxygen. It fills us. It fuels us. It gives us life.

Fear of Success

When I turned down that out-of-the-blue book deal all those years ago, I would be lying if I didn't admit that a large part of the relief I felt was also the knowledge that I wouldn't have to put myself out there in such a public way...at least not yet.

Delaying the success that I so desperately desired gave me comfort. How could that be?

The fear of being in the spotlight, of going after what you want and succeeding at it, is also very uncomfortable. It wasn't something that I fully comprehended when I started my career, but as my platforms grew, I realized that with more eyes watching come more criticism, judgment, and opinions. Punting the proverbial "book deal" ball down the field meant that I wouldn't have to deal with putting myself out there in such a public way for a while.

We have talked a lot about the fear and consequences of failure...but what about the fear and consequences of success? What about all of the people who hold back from going after what they really want because they are terrified of dealing with the increased pressure and scrutiny?

When we think about making critical life decisions, we cannot ignore our deeply ingrained tendencies to avoid anything that brings about discomfort or the anticipation of future pain. This is how our brain works. Understanding how this may impact our ability to say yes to the things that we want or even convince ourselves that denying those opportunities are best for us, however, is paramount.

Getting gutsy and achieving your goals inevitably will mean moving beyond your comfort zone into unfamiliar territory. For some, it may mean taking on additional responsibilities or widening your sphere of influence. For others, it may mean stepping away from public platforms altogether and pursuing a different, but no less daunting, version of success (with heaps of judgment over your change of course).

Simply put, pursuing your unique definition of success is scary, and it has consequences.

So what is the fear of success, how does it manifest in our lives, and how do we ensure it doesn't cloud our decision-making or keep us from saying yes to the right things?

Signs you might be struggling with the fear of success include the following:

- Setting low expectations for yourself or failing to reach set goals
- Denying yourself opportunities for advancement or promotion
- Procrastinating, avoiding making a decision, or putting things off until the last minute
- Quitting when you are on the verge of success
- Self-sabotaging or intentionally placing obstacles in your own way
- Diminishing your own accomplishments or credibility; using subordinate language

The fear of success isn't so much about success itself, but rather the potential consequences that come with it. Some of this fear is hardwired in; however, much of it is socially constructed and/or culturally conditioned. There are both innate and learned factors at play.

For many people, achieving success means disrupting existing power structures and societal dynamics. Social conditioning is one way that power dynamics are upheld and perpetuated.

For example, some people experience the fear of success because they anticipate very real societal or relational repercussions. Avoiding success out of fear of those repercussions is known as "backlash avoidance" and is more common among women than men.[1] Studies have also found that women avoid behaviors like self-promotion because it does not align with traditional gender roles.[2]

In this way, fearing the repercussions of success leads us to do things that aren't in our own best interest. For example, one of the most common and subtle ways that we undercut our own credibility is through the use of subordinate language. There is a very good chance that you are doing this without even realizing it.

It often sounds like this:

I am so sorry to bother you. I just wanted to follow up on our conversation.

I just wanted to drop this off. I am sorry for any disruption.

Back in 2015, Ellen Petry Leanse, a former Apple and Google employee, shook up the tech world when she launched

1. Corinne A. Moss-Racusin and Laurie A. Rudman, "Disruptions in Women's Self-Promotion: The Backlash Avoidance Model," *Psychology of Women Quarterly* 34, no. 2 (2010): 186–202, doi: 10.1111/j.1471-6402.2010.01561.x.

2. Natasza Kosakowska-Berezecka et al., "Self-Presentation Strategies, Fear of Success and Anticipation of Future Success among University and High School Students," *Frontiers in Psychology*, October 27, 2017, https://www.frontiersin.org/articles/10.3389 /fpsyg.2017.01884/full. The backlash avoidance model suggests women insufficiently self-promote because they fear backlash for behavior that is incongruent with traditional gender roles. Avoiding self-promoting behavior is also potentially related to associating success with negative consequences.

a campaign to strike the word "just" from women's vocabularies. She realized that her colleagues used the word as a subtle message of subordination or deference, and it was holding them back.[3]

When used in phrases like "just checking in" or "just following up," the word softens the request in order to be perceived as more amenable and pleasing. Throwing in the word "just" makes someone seem softer, smaller, and less threatening or confrontational. For women, this means adhering to socially constructed gender norms.

In the small-business world, many of us have been on a mission for years to eliminate this term from our vocabulary and transform the way that we talk about ourselves and the work that we do. When used alongside parts of our identity, it becomes even more damaging...And again, most of us don't even realize that we're doing it.

I am "just" a _____.

I am "just" a photographer.

I am "just" a teacher.

I am "just" a stay-at-home parent.

---

3. Ellen Petry Leanse, "The One Word You Should Strike from Your Vocabulary Stat to Sound More Confident," Business Insider, December 18, 2019, https://www.businessinsider.com/former-google-exec-says-this-word-can-damage-your-credibility-2015-6?IR=T.

Whew! This gets me all fired up. I wish you could see me furiously typing away on my keyboard with that angry mama-bear look in my eyes. I need you to hear me when I say...

You are not "just" anything.

The work that you do matters. Your contributions matter. We need to eradicate this adverb from being used in our vocabulary like this. Stop downgrading the work that you do by throwing "just" immediately before your title.

Language matters. It impacts how we feel about ourselves and how others perceive our self-confidence. If you swap out the word "just" for any one of its synonyms, it becomes even clearer how language like this is harmful.

I am "no more than" a photographer.

I am "at most" a teacher.

I am "nothing but" a stay-at-home parent.

Yikes. Isn't that awful? Let's cut it out, kick it to the curb, and hold one another accountable to stop saying it. We need to quit diminishing ourselves by using language that undercuts our value and reduces our contributions.

Whether we are aware of it or not, often our fear of success can stand in the way of us living happy, fulfilled, and impactful lives. If you feel like this fear is holding you back from saying yes to opportunities that are right for you, there are things you can do to overcome it.

Begin by asking yourself the following questions:

- What is it about being successful that scares me?
- Do I associate success with negative outcomes? What are they and why?
- What are the good things that could happen if I am successful? Who could I help? What positive impact could I make?

Work on reframing your limiting beliefs about success while simultaneously addressing any potential outcomes that scare you. Avoid discounting the positive potential outcomes. Talk with a friend, family member, or partner about it. Get additional perspectives, clarity, and support.

If you still find yourself unable to move forward, bring it up with a mental health professional. By now you know that I am a huge champion for therapy, and especially if this fear is deeply debilitating for you, start there. Getting a trained, outside perspective can sometimes make all the difference.

CHAPTER 8

MAKE YOURSELF PROUD

"I don't know how you do it. You are Superwoman. You have a business, two little kids, a happy marriage, a busy personal life. I can't even empty my inbox or remember to water my plants."

The minute the words were out of my friend's mouth, I wanted to hurl. I have never felt like more of an imposter than I did at that moment.

Superwoman? I am not Superwoman. I am the furthest thing from it.

I am falling apart. I am letting everyone in my life down. I feel like I can't do anything right. The multitude of identities that I juggle at any given moment makes me feel like I might spontaneously combust.

As if one minute I am sipping an oat milk latte and the next I am—*poof*—a giant pile of rainbow confetti scattered across the coffee shop floor. It might not be physically possible, but I would not be surprised if by some miracle it happened anyway.

What's worse is that even if I could somehow be Superwoman, I wouldn't want to be. I do not want all of that responsibility.

I want help. I want a break. I want the freedom to change my mind. I want to have the freedom to make mistakes. I want to be loved even with my imperfections, loved for who I truly am. I don't want to hide my brokenness, my humanity, under a flashy red cape.

And yet...that was precisely what I had been doing. Perhaps there is some part of you that has been doing this too.

Maybe you are trying to be everything to everyone, all of the time. Maybe you are working so hard to not let anyone down that you unintentionally let yourself down in the process.

Maybe you put on your cape a long time ago and convinced the world that you too were a superhero...because you were taught to see that as your role to fill. Maybe you were conditioned to believe that anything less than perfection was unacceptable—that disappointing your parents, your friends, or your community was a fate worse than death.

That cuts a little too deep, doesn't it? I know that for some of you it will, and I promise to bring you out on the other side. If you have carried these concerns for far too long, this is your opportunity to lay them down.

When my friend made that comment about being Superwoman to me, she meant it as a compliment and yet it made me realize that I was losing myself in the pursuit of saving everyone else. I was trying to be too many people all at once. I was trying to do too many things at the same time.

I was so deeply afraid that if I wasn't the perfect mom, the best friend, the loving partner, the inspiring leader, then I wasn't enough. I was terrified that if I didn't live up to who I should be, then I was the failure that I fought so hard to avoid becoming. Oh, and who I "should" be was everything to everyone all the time.

But here's the thing—something powerful happens when you ditch your cape.

Something fundamentally shifts when you let those impossibly high expectations come crashing down and you tell the world that you refuse to play by its rules anymore. Something clicks when you stop seeing yourself as the supporting character in everyone else's life and you start being the author of your own story.

No longer is the summation of your identity watered down into a highlight reel of greatness. You can be messy, dynamic, flawed, and no less extraordinary. No longer do you shrink down, swallow your words, or shift your entire being to be more palatable for the comfort of others. You step into the gifts you were given, and you reclaim the calling that is rightfully yours.

When you abandon being the superhero that you think the world expects you to be, you are one step closer to being the true champion that you have needed all along. In order to uncover that version of yourself, you have to come to terms with an uncomfortable realization:

To be your own hero, you must have the courage to let other people down.

Making Yourself Proud

After college graduation, I ditched the prospect of a traditional corporate career to become a full-time photographer. People were shocked. To spend four years getting an Ivy League degree and then, by their standards, choose to "throw it all away" and pursue something they perceived to be a less prestigious risk baffled them.

However, I knew in my bones that my calling wasn't to hustle in an ivory tower overlooking the Manhattan skyline. It is a wonderful dream, don't get me wrong, but it was meant for someone else. I wanted to wake up with a camera in my hand, to work beneath golden sunsets with people who were madly and irrevocably in love.

I wanted a career that set me free to be my truest self.

At the time, there were many who thought I was making

a mistake…to turn down the opportunity to climb a respectable corporate ladder and instead set out to construct my own from foraged bits of wood and a DIY construction manual as I built a business on my own terms seemed foolhardy.

When you spend four years of your life going down one road, working for a piece of paper that grants you entry to a land of opportunity like an elusive golden ticket, you keep on driving forward…right?

Well, not me. I took that diploma, folded it in half (*lovingly, of course—it was wildly expensive and I had all the obscenely large student loans to prove it*), and stuck it in the sun visor above the windshield as I veered ferociously in the opposite direction.

Why? It was because of a comment my grandmother had made to me one year earlier.

It was a single sentence in one of the final conversations that we had together before she passed away. And to be honest, I am not even sure that she meant it to impact me so greatly. It was more of an automatic response than it was some elaborate thought-out speech.

She had been battling stage-four lung cancer for several months, and when it was clear that our time together was dwindling, I took the train home from college in Philadelphia to spend one last afternoon with her.

I still remember the aching sadness that pressed upon me as I walked into her house.

It felt like one of those moments in a movie where you

know that the next scene is going to destroy you...so you try, futilely, to find some nonexistent pause button to prevent the inevitable from unfolding.

You stretch out every second as long as you can. You firmly grasp the very hand of time with an unrelenting grip and white knuckles, as if your sheer willpower will hold it back from ticking onward. And only when it becomes clear that your time together must come to a close do you offer up a hesitant, tear-filled goodbye.

My version of "white-knuckling" the rope in this tug-of-war with the inevitable was to ask her dozens of questions in endless succession. I wanted to squeeze every last drop of meaning from this moment, and so...with her hand in mine, I asked all of the things that I have ever wanted to ask.

What were her fondest memories? Where was she hiding her secret recipes? What was the meaning of life and the key to a successful marriage? Why did she nickname me after a local Baltimore beer—and not a particularly good one at that?

It was a good day. We laughed. We cried. We munched on saltine crackers listening to Frank Sinatra. We spent hours sitting together at her kitchen table before it was time for her to rest.

I stood, collected her glass of ginger ale, and started to walk over to place it in the sink, when I froze. A feeling of panic rose up within me. I don't know why, but I felt desperate to end what could be our last long conversation with her stamp of approval.

I longed for one final affirmation that I was growing into the woman that she dreamt for me to be...So I looked over at her and said, "I really hope that I make you proud, Mom-Mom."

Her eyes met mine.

I was hoping to hear her say something to the effect of "You already do" or a comforting "You always will," but she didn't. If she had, I wouldn't be writing this story, let alone this book, because nothing fundamental in my heart would have changed. This moment wouldn't have eaten away at me for months afterward as I unpacked what it truly meant.

Without her response, I am not sure I would have had the courage to take my photography business full-time after graduation and brush off the judgment of others. I definitely wouldn't have declared war on the dog-eat-dog, cutthroat competition of the small-business world. I wouldn't have publicly shared my journey—my benign brain tumor diagnosis, neurosurgery, recovery, infertility, and IVF—with tens of thousands of strangers on the internet.

No freaking way...

Had my grandmother simply offered me one more dopamine hit of validation woven into her expression of approval, my life would look vastly different. I would have stayed the course. I might have even taken a corporate job after graduation and set my camera down for good.

I genuinely thought she would affirm me as one normally does when the other person is visibly feeling insecure and yearning for validation. Instead, she responded by turning the statement back on me.

With that familiar fiery tone, that spark of sass that had made my very petite, five-foot-tall grandmother a legendary force to behold, she said,

"Make yourself proud," and paused.

Then she added, "And *that* will make me proud, Natty Boh."

Reframe Your Goals

When you set out to make yourself proud, even at the risk of letting other people down, it requires you to reevaluate nearly everything in your life...including your goals. Many of us shape our vision of the future around what we think will make other people happy, and it isn't until we begin to see our lives with this new perspective that our priorities shift.

Nearly every self-help book that I have ever opened and countless keynote talks I have heard over the years mention goals and goal setting. I understand why. How can you possibly be successful in life, or make yourself proud, for that matter, if you don't know what you want or have a road map to get there? Right?

Goals serve a meaningful purpose in helping us to get what we want from life. They are effective. They have been proven time and time again to work.

Several studies have shown that when we train ourselves to

focus on what we want in life and we work toward achieving it, the brain consequently rewires itself. It makes that vision of the future an essential part of our identity, bringing our behaviors into alignment to positively drive us forward. If we reach the goal, we are rewarded with feelings of pleasure and fulfillment, and if we don't, our brain keeps nudging us along until we achieve it.[1]

There is so much good that comes out of setting and achieving goals. I agree with that wholeheartedly. However, in all of the tips and tricks that are shared to help you get to where you want to go, rarely does anyone want to address the question of whether the final destination you have in your mind is even the right one.

It feels like everyone is out in the world with a megaphone shouting, "Go after your goals!" or giving you a framework for achieving them—but very few people are asking you the questions that I believe matter the most. For example, I am sure that all of us at one point or another have been asked questions like these:

Where do you see yourself in a year?

What do you want to achieve?

What are your long-term career or personal aspirations?

---

1. Madhuleena Roy Chowdhury, "The Science & Psychology of Goal-Setting 101," PositivePsychology.com, May 2, 2019, https://positivepsychology.com /goal-setting-psychology/.

They are on nearly every college application that you complete. They are a part of nearly every traditional job interview you take. When it comes to casting a vision of the future, we like to focus on the "what" of it all.

There are several ways in which this often leads even the most successful people astray. They place achievement on a pedestal. They run in the wrong direction. They sacrifice the things that matter for the ones that don't. They lose the people who they love most in their lives by placing profit or popularity above purpose.

I feel a little like I am Taylor Swift at the moment, singing, "I think I've seen this film before, and I didn't like the ending."

The uncomfortable truth is that many of the most successful people in the world are miserable. They have everything and yet nothing that matters. The hard lesson that we often learn is this:

Goals mean nothing if they aren't leading you in the right direction.

You can check every box, receive every award, conquer every challenge, earn all of the applause you can imagine...but if you aren't going after the right things, none of it matters.

So how do we keep that from happening? Perhaps try asking yourself a different question. Before thinking about *what* you want to accomplish, dig a little deeper and ask,

- In the future, how do I want to feel?
- What does a life in alignment with that feeling mean to me?
- What would success look like in that scenario?

Questions like these give us clarity into how we want to feel when we achieve the success that our goals will surely lead us toward.

It reduces the risk that we pursue someone else's definition of success or begin running down a road that was never going to lead us to a fulfilling life. By directing our attention not toward accolades or achievement but rather toward how we want to experience the world, it gives us a different perspective.

For some of us, that might not change the big dreams that we have or the goals that we have set. However, for others, it could have the power to change everything. It is important that if you do find yourself taking a big leap or making a giant change, you brace yourself for a multitude of opinions.

Disappointing others or receiving disapproval is not only the result of our failures. Sometimes it also happens when we go after our dreams and even when we succeed.

"Why Can't They Just Be Happy for Me?"

Have you ever asked yourself this question? When something good happens—whether it is dating someone new, moving to a new city, or accomplishing a giant dream—it is often shocking how people, even those closest to you, can be unsupportive or even dismissive of our success.

So often we think about letting others down through the lens of our mistakes or our weaknesses, but sometimes this happens in response to things we are proud of.

I have seen scenarios like this play out a lot in the small-business world. The minute someone decides they want to start a side hustle, pick up freelance work, or quit their corporate job to do their own thing, it rattles the people closest to them and draws criticism from all fronts.

It is often the ones they trust the most who are the first to question or criticize their decision or withdraw emotionally. There is even a joke among small-business owners that "no one will support you like your internet friends who have never even met you."

Why might that be? I believe there are two common reasons.

The first reason those closest to you might be hesitant or discouraging is because they don't want to see you get hurt. Their concern often comes from a genuinely good place, but it's delivered in a way that has an anything but good effect.

Those who love you may see you taking a risk and they are terrified of you experiencing pain or hardship as a result of that choice. If they could prevent you from experiencing hardship of any kind, they would.

This results in them projecting their own fears and allowing their desire to protect you outweigh their ability to support you. They may even do this without realizing it.

It often comes across as though they disagree with your decision, think you are making a foolish mistake, or, most painfully, that they don't believe you are capable of success. A lot of the time, however, especially for those who have your best interests at heart, their opposition is a protection mechanism. While their intent might be good, that doesn't stop the impact of their words from having negative consequences.

The second reason is the most important in regard to this particular conversation because it plays out beyond the people who love you. It's critical to understand in all of your future interactions.

Human beings are mirrors for one another.

As social creatures, we are constantly comparing ourselves to our peers. When someone's thoughts or behaviors align with our own, it appeases our insecurities and strengthens our self-esteem.

When you go after your dreams and step beyond what is safe and familiar, it causes other people to reflect on their own life choices and belief systems. When someone looks at you, they see aspects of themselves reflected back. Your choices make them think about their choices. Your values make them analyze their own values. The way you navigate the world is directly compared and contrasted with their own lived experiences.

So when you take a risk, pursue a dream, speak your

mind, or divert from what they themselves have done, it can challenge their entire worldview. That is a dangerous thing.

Think of the beliefs that make up someone's worldview like a giant game of Jenga. Just in case you aren't familiar with the game, it is where you stack block upon block upon block to create a tower formation and then proceed to remove blocks from the center one by one.

When the tower is completely whole and solid from top to bottom without any gaps, it is the strongest. This is precisely what the human brain desires—comfort, safety, stability. As you proceed to pull blocks out, like removing foundational beliefs from the very core of a person, you create vulnerabilities that threaten to topple the entire tower.

In the case of the small-business example, if someone has spent their entire life working a corporate job, believing that it is the only path to stability and success, and you prove that wrong by succeeding at the very thing they have always believed wasn't possible, they start to wonder what other beliefs of theirs could also be wrong.

You become the threat—simply by existing.

By going after your dream, you bring their own career decisions into question. An area of their life that once felt certain is now full of questions.

Did I make the wrong choice to stay at my job? Would I have been happier starting my own business?

Without realizing it, your very existence becomes a

psychological threat that is directly at odds with the comfort their brain desperately craves.

As you can imagine, this doesn't always go over well.

It can manifest in a multitude of ways, but the underlying emotion is often fear. They don't hate you. They are just afraid of what you represent.

When faced with a situation like this, it is often easier for someone to reject and dismiss the opposition than it is to confront the possibility that they themselves could be wrong.

If that opposing belief is right, then my belief must be wrong. Therefore, all of my other existing beliefs could be incorrect as well...and that could crumble my entire worldview.

They might feel defensive when your stance is different from their own. They may confront you about your words or actions to assure themselves that you are in the wrong—not them.

What is important to remember is that how someone responds to you living out your values says more about them than it does about you. There are a multitude of reasons why someone might not support your success or the positive change as you grow into a better version of yourself.

Regardless of what you do, say, or even don't do or don't say, you cannot control how other people feel about you. There will always be someone who is at odds with who you are, what you believe, how you live, who you love, or how you view the world.

The people-pleasing perfectionist in all of us is downright terrified by this possibility. This is the very thing we are bending over backward to avoid, right? This is the worst-case scenario that we sacrifice our own well-being for and that we second-guess our every move to prevent from happening...and yet...it likely already has.

To someone else, you are the friend who they cannot forgive, you are the partner who broke their heart, you are the boss who let them go, or you are the scoundrel who spoiled the ending of their favorite TV show, right?

And yet, that is okay.

If you have a pulse, I am willing to bet that someone doesn't like you. If you have ever used your voice, I have a good feeling that at least one person out there doesn't like something you have had to say. This can either hold you hostage in fear, causing you to expend all of your energy as you bend over backward to win others over...or it can free you to see the truth that has been in front of you all along.

Letting someone else down doesn't mean that you are bad, unlovable, a failure, or any of the other lies that you have been told or have told yourself that disappointing others will make you. You are still beautifully and remarkably you regardless of their perception.

As uncomfortable as it is to accept, you have to be comfortable with others disagreeing with you on your values, convictions, boundaries, decisions, and actions—and lack thereof.

Let people judge you. Let them disapprove of you. It is not your job to convince the world that you are worth loving. You are inherently worthy whether they see it or not.

The moment that we release our need to control how other people feel about us, when we come to terms with the fact that their opinions, approval, and validation of who we are is not our responsibility, we can stop striving to be loved and start truly living.

Becoming the Writer of Our Own Story

> *Your job throughout your entire life is to*
> *disappoint as many people as it takes to*
> *avoid disappointing yourself.*
> —GLENNON DOYLE

The moment we stop trying to be the person the world wants us to be, we enter a new season of our lives. When we confront the inevitabilities of all the things we have been trying to outrun and all the fears we have bent over backward to avoid seeing come true, we are finally ready to become the writer of our own story.

So what does this mean precisely? How is this different from the role we assumed before?

You must be the one to write the next chapter.

If you have been ruled by the opinions of others, this is the moment you take the pen from their hands and place it confidently in your own. You take on the authorship of your future. You take responsibility for how the plot unfolds in the years to come.

Rather than looking outward at who the world expects you to be and striving for that impossible ideal until it robs you of everything that you are, you first look within. You begin by asking yourself, What is it that I need? Who is it that I need?

With a pen in hand, you write a new future. One in which you embrace your imperfections, your past failures, and your future mistakes. You put yourself first—perhaps for the first time in a long time—even if it makes your fingers tremble. You heal. You grieve. You ask for help. You give yourself the safe space you worked so hard to be for everyone else.

You put your oxygen mask on first before helping others in that moment the plane experiences a change in cabin pressure... You know the metaphor! It is brutally overdone, but darn if it isn't accurate here. Yeah?

You ditch the cape. You step into a future that only you can write. A future that only you cannot wait to live.

What it really comes down to is that you write your story without the fear of letting other people down. You allow your voice to rise above the criticism, to drown out the whispers, to echo in every valley until it drives out the darkness that once lingered there.

When we rise up to become the hero of our own story, we finally accept the truth about disappointing others. It isn't just a possibility that might happen. It is a guarantee in a life lived with purpose.

Even if we desire to be selfless, altruistic, compassionate human beings on an unprecedented scale, we must first treat ourselves with that same respect.

We help no one by burning out, by allowing our inner flame to be smothered under the weight of the world's unattainable ideals. We are of no value to others when we sacrifice our own needs endlessly from a position of fear, doubt, or insecurity. We make no impact when we tear ourselves apart emotionally, bending over backward to avoid letting anyone down.

The truth is that if you spend your entire life focused on avoiding other people's disappointment, then you are guaranteed to disappoint the person who matters most.

By honoring ourselves, we are bound to accrue criticism, judgment, and heaps of unsolicited opinions. We must choose to love, respect, and prioritize ourselves regardless. We must fight for ourselves fiercely and unapologetically. We must become the heroes that we needed when we were younger. We must become the healers that our souls inherently deserve. It must begin with us.

Honoring Younger You

I went back and forth on whether to share the story earlier in this chapter about that final conversation with my grandmother. You see, it is one that I have held very close to my heart for over a decade now, and there is still a part of me that wonders what she would think of the person that I have become.

Even after all this time, her opinion genuinely still matters that much to me. I can't help but hear her voice play on repeat in my head on days when the doubt creeps in.

Make yourself proud.

It is a call to look within yourself and honor your own needs, a charge to hold space for the most vulnerable parts of you. It is a reminder to set goals that honor how you desire to feel in the future. It is a rallying cry to keep showing up and fighting to be the person that you were created to be.

Free from striving. Free from shrinking back to make others feel more comfortable. Free from chasing someone else's desire for your life. Free from so much of what holds us back.

For a moment, I want you to imagine that we are rewinding all the way to the earlier portion of this chapter at that kitchen table in my grandmother's house and swapping out the main characters.

Pretend for a moment that my story is now, in fact, *your* story.

But rather than a granddaughter and her grandmother, it's two versions of you separated only by time. A younger you and an older you, engaged in one final conversation. If you had the chance at the end of this life to speak to yourself as a child, what would you say?

What would be the advice that you'd give to yourself?

What stories would you be able to tell yourself from the years that you walked this earth? What risks did you take, what lessons did you learn, what legacy are you leaving behind?

Would you tell yourself to make *yourself* proud—to be true to your values, to fight for what you believe in with all of your heart, to take risks and live with bold, brave, and boundless courage?

Would you advise the younger you to love yourself in a world that is so committed to benefiting from your doubts and insecurities? Would you affirm the greatness you see within that growing mind, the potential that you were so quick to see in others but failed to recognize in yourself?

Perhaps it is time you write those words down and truly take on the role of the author of your own story. Perhaps it is time you share the words that you would speak to your younger self if you were granted one final conversation. Perhaps these are the very words that you also need to hear at this precise moment.

Oftentimes, empowering advice and unconditional love are two things that we are so quick to give to others freely and yet just as likely to withhold from ourselves. This is an exercise in honoring a younger you, in taking your own advice, and in imagining a future where you truly live to the fullest.

Do you want to hear the words that I would share if I were to sit at that kitchen table? Do you want to know what I would do if the roles were reversed and I was not the recipient of my grandmother's wisdom but rather the one giving it?

Here is what I would share with younger me:

Don't wait until your life is over to begin living it.

Time will slip through your fingers if you let it. It is the only thing you can never get more of...the only thing that you can never get back. Don't waste a second of it. Cherish it. Honor it. Seize it.

There is no award for making yourself smaller, staying stuck, or remaining silent in the face of things that matter. There is no gold medal for never getting started. There is no impact without action. So move. You heard me—go! Get after it!

Stop being so afraid to disappoint others that you end up disappointing yourself. You are deserving of so much more.

Stop hesitating. Stop swallowing your words. Stop second-guessing your choices. Stop dimming your light and shrinking back into a shell of who you truly are. Offer yourself the same love and encouragement that you give to others so freely.

You are strong. You are brave. You are a genuine soul and a vivacious spirit. The world desperately needs what you have to offer.

Hold your head up high. Wear what you want. Say what you want. Lie down in the pouring rain if it makes you happy. Go dancing—often. Surprise people. Surprise yourself. Stop waiting for the weekend. Stop waiting for permission. Stop waiting for what's next. Live now. Leap now. Take risks. Dream again. Be your own cheerleader.

This life is yours. When are you finally going to live it?

It has been over a decade since my grandmother uttered the words "Make yourself proud," and while I am not quite sure that I am there yet, I am closer than I have ever been. My hope is that by the end of this book, you are closer too.

It is going to take guts and perhaps a few more tears, but we're on our way there together.

To write your own letter to your younger self, visit https://nataliefranke.com/letter to download a printable template.

CHAPTER 9

GETTING UNSTUCK

My son, Huey, is obsessed with Play-Doh.

The sheer amount of rainbow and glitter-infused dough that we have in our house, including in places that it doesn't belong, would shock you.

Okay, it would shock *some* of you. I have no doubt there are cupboards full of slime or kinetic sand out there that would rival the collection that I am talking about in our home, but I digress...

One day, while I was attempting to vacuum up dried dough shavings from the gaps between our scuffed-up century-old wood floors, a thought came to mind.

Who invented Play-Doh? Which brilliant soul conceptualized and created one of the most successful toys in history? As I ran my vacuum over the same spot for the third time, I was genuinely curious who to credit, or perhaps blame, for the stuff.

A quick Google search later, I was surprised by what I learned.

Play-Doh was never designed to be a toy for children. It was not even a thought in anyone's mind when the product was originally created and brought to market. What was the purpose of it?

Play-Doh was originally used to take soot off of wallpaper. The soft, pliable dough was a reliable cleaning substance for decades until the transition away from coal heating in the 1950s meant that coal, and therefore wallpaper cleaner, was no longer in high demand.

This dealt a devastating blow to Kutol Products, who had become the largest wallpaper-cleaner manufacturer in existence. They feared that there was no future for the product in a world without soot. In an attempt to change the trajectory of the declining company, Joseph McVicker was brought in to save Kutol Products from potential bankruptcy. Shortly after taking on the challenge, McVicker had a conversation with his sister-in-law and then nursery school teacher, Kay Zufall, about the issue.

Remembering an article that she had read about dough being used for modeling projects, Kay brought the material into her classroom to see what the children thought. It was a hit. The nursery school children absolutely loved it, and she suggested that Joseph pivot the product and call the substance Play-Doh.[1]

Fast-forward many decades later, and it has become one of the most successful toys ever invented...a toy that was never intended to be a toy at all.

We have talked quite a bit in this book about how when we confine ourselves to living a life that is expected and approved by others, we hold ourselves back from truly living at all. Striving for validation and bending over backward for approval keep us chasing after what we think other people want rather than going after dreams of our own.

We have also established that when we are fearful of disappointing the people around us or when we excessively worry about judgment and criticism, our mind gets stuck and is unable to take decisive action. Our brain's behavioral inhibition system becomes engaged, and it may even fail to deactivate, thereby inhibiting us from moving forward.

Getting stuck once is frustrating. Remaining stuck in a feedback loop of fear and insecurity is like living in a prison that we ourselves have built. It is deeply debilitating and emotionally draining to exist that way day in and day out.

So how do we break free from those patterns that are holding us hostage?

---

1. David Kindy, "The Accidental Invention of Play-Doh," *Smithsonian Magazine*, November 12, 2019, https://www.smithsonianmag.com/innovation /accidental-invention-play-doh-180973527/#:~:text=Joseph%20McVicker%20was%20 trying%20to,into%20all%20kinds%20of%20shapes.

How do we transition from a momentary pause to being propelled forward into meaningful action? In this chapter, we are going to discuss several strategies for getting unstuck and the techniques that will help us stay that way. Let's start with failure.

The Batter's Box

What if we cultivated environments in our lives that embraced failure? Rather than tucking our mistakes away or hiding our defeat, what if we gave failure the floor? It's a concept that feels counterintuitive, and yet for many, it serves as the very mindset they credit with their success.

Sara Blakely, the founder and CEO of Spanx, attributes her ability to reframe failure as one of the keys to her success. When she was a child, her father encouraged her to fail.

Growing up, he would ask Sara, "What have you failed at this week?" That single question changed her mindset at an early age. She began to see failure not as an outcome, but as a stepping stone on the road to success.

Sara Blakely's early career failures are arguably what led her to the billion-dollar idea that has become the household name we know today. She said she wanted to be a lawyer but did terribly on the LSAT—twice. She moved on to a new dream and headed to Disney World, trying out to be the character Goofy, but she wasn't tall enough to get the part. She then sold fax machines for seven years in corporate America.

It was then that she struggled finding undergarments that met her needs, and she cut the feet out of a pair of control-top pantyhose to create the first prototype for Spanx. Her invention launched shapewear into the mainstream.

There were a whole host of hurdles that she faced in those initial years of entrepreneurship, but she persevered. Each failure launched her forward toward her future success.[2]

Imagine if Sara Blakely had continued wearing her control-top pantyhose and never tried turning her invention into a business because she worried about what other people might think. Imagine if she allowed the opinions of early investors, who turned her down for having zero entrepreneurial experience, to stop her from pressing onward.

Reframing our perspective on failure can have a transformative effect on our trajectory.

So often we feel pressure to craft and share a version of ourselves that is free from flaws, shortcomings, errors, and any glimmer of inadequacy. We share our filtered faces in curated clips of highlight-reel memories while tucking away the messy moments that actually matter.

In doing so, we hide the very parts of us that are uniquely human. This puts perfection on a pedestal and raises the stakes for anyone stepping out into the unknown. The less we see failure, the less we remember that it is an inevitable part of

---

2. Robert Frank, "Billionaire Sara Blakely Says Secret to Success Is Failure," CNBC, October 16, 2013, https://www.cnbc.com/2013/10/16/billionaire-sara-blakely-says-secret-to-success-is-failure.html.

life. By removing it from our field of view, we forget just how common and necessary it is on the road to success.

Reframing our relationship with failure will take us places that chasing perfection never will.

Imagine for a moment that from here on, you set aside time every week to list out all of the risks you had taken and things you have failed at. From the tiny whoopsie-daisies to the epic public disasters, you document them and raise a glass in their honor. No shame allowed—there is only room for radical curiosity and the wisdom that comes from taking your best shot.

What do you think might happen?

This not-so-hypothetical practice transformed my entire life.

A few years ago, shortly after the community I co-founded was acquired by a tech startup, I got a brand-new boss. This boss, Dan Visnick, was impressive. He had a mile-long list of accomplishments and had worked at some of the most successful companies in Silicon Valley.

Needless to say, I was nervous. Genuinely nervous. As a chief executive, he would be fundamentally responsible for building the team and ensuring the success of the entire marketing organization. That came with a lot of pressure.

I will never forget our first team meeting when Dan looked around the room and asked, "Do you know how many swings on average it takes a major league baseball player to hit a home run?"

Of all the things that I thought he might ask, this certainly wasn't one of them.

"The number isn't actually the important part...It's the fact that you can't hit a home run without swinging the bat. And baseball players who get a hit three out of ten at bats are extremely successful. Of those that they hit, only a fraction of them make it all the way to the stands. It takes a lot of at bats to hit even a single home run."

This concept is what inspired Dan to institute the weekly practice of the Batter's Box—where members of the team present new initiatives they are trying, tests they are running, or mistakes they have made in the pursuit of chasing that elusive home run. This practice of honoring the journey and celebrating the failures that bring us closer to success resulted in a culture of psychological safety.

Rather than being reprimanded for failure, employees are encouraged to keep getting up to swing the bat. As a result, they take more risks, innovate frequently, think more creatively, and simply perform better. That is the precise mindset that leads to success.

When you make failure the enemy, you give it power. The same can be said about fearing judgment, criticism, and other people's opinions. By embracing its inevitable existence rather than fearing it, you grant yourself permission to continue moving forward anyway.

If you don't get up to swing the bat, you'll never hit a home run.

Are you going to strike out? Of course you will. You'll probably strike out quite a lot. However, if you keep showing up, eventually you might just knock it out of the park.

This has also been the case for so many of the most popular books in history. Many of the authors who have become household names were rejected more than once when submitting their manuscripts.

Stephen King's book *Carrie* received 30 rejections from publishers. Kathryn Stockett's manuscript, *The Help*, was turned down 60 times before getting an offer. And my favorite? *Chicken Soup for the Soul* was rejected a whopping 144 times.[3]

Think of all the bestsellers that were never printed because an author simply chose to stop submitting. This number, although huge, I have no doubt, still pales in comparison to the number of books that were never even written because the author allowed their doubts and fears to stand in the way of putting their pen to the page.

Stop allowing fear of failure or of what people will think of you when you fail to keep you from continuing to try.

The Power of Play

When was the last time that you played? That you simply had fun for the thrill of it? That you did something enjoyable

---

3. Emily Temple, "The Most Rejected Books of All Time," Literary Hub, December 22, 2017, https://lithub.com/the-most-rejected-books-of-all-time/.

without the pressure of the world watching? At its core, play is radical curiosity brought to life.

As children, we are encouraged to play, and it serves a significant function in our personal development. As we age, however, play becomes less and less a part of our lives—we trade toys for taxes and recess for brief walks to grab coffee between back-to-back calls.

The emotional freedom we feel in our youth is replaced by pressure—the pressure to perform, the pressure to fit in, the pressure to succeed. The stakes are raised with each added responsibility that adulthood brings with it.

What if I told you that reincorporating play into your life could help to get you unstuck and empower you to feel more equipped to navigate all that pressure? It is true. Play can do that and a whole lot more.

Play impacts our brain on a neurobiological level. When we engage in play, our brain releases a rush of endogenous opioids and cannabinoids impacting key areas of the brain including the prefrontal cortex, striatum, and amygdala.[4] This shift in our neurochemistry can rewire our brain to function better in all contexts—allowing us to expand the number of operations we can run, entertain new possibilities, and make better predictions about what could happen next.[5]

---

4. Stephen M. Siviy and Jaak Panksepp, "In Search of the Neurobiological Substrates for Social Playfulness in Mammalian Brains," *Neuroscience & Biobehavioral Reviews* 35, no. 9 (October 2011), https://www.sciencedirect.com/science/article/abs/pii /S0149763411000492?via=ihub.

5. Andrew Huberman, "Using Play to Rewire & Improve Your Brain," *Huberman Lab Podcast*, accessed July 21, 2022, https://hubermanlab.com/using-play-to-rewire -and-improve-your-brain/.

In a metaphorical sense, imagine that your brain operates like a GPS in high-pressure situations. It gives you the most efficient path from point A to point B. Engaging play is like switching the GPS into a slightly different mode that effectively broadens its routing capability, allowing it to show you a multitude of different avenues that you could explore along the way.

Play enables you to expand beyond your comfort zone, try out new roles, and experiment with different modes of operation. It optimizes your brain to be more flexible and creative.

When you are feeling stuck, leveraging play can improve your cognitive function, enhance your creativity, and expand your framework of thinking. It removes the pressure of performance and lowers the stakes such that you can engage in challenges from a different perspective. Play sets aside the expectations of who you "should" be and removes the immense strain of adulthood, replacing it with an environment of possibilities, creativity, exploration, and self-discovery.

Play can also prompt your imagination, helping you problem solve and think outside the box. When play involves other people, it has the ability to improve your relationships and increase feelings of connectedness.

There is extensive evidence to show that when you engage in play as a child, it contributes to your ability to navigate an ever-changing social, emotional, and cognitive landscape as an adult.[6] Reincorporating this practice into your life at a later

6. Stephen M. Siviy, "A Brain Motivated to Play: Insights into the Neurobiology of Playfulness," *Behaviour* 153, nos. 6–7 (2016): 819–844, doi: 10.1163/1568539X-00003349.

stage as well has significant benefits. Let's talk about how to do it.

There are a few key things to keep in mind when leveraging play:

- **Keep it low stakes.** The stress-free aspect of play is critical. Engaging in a low-stakes environment means that winning or losing is of little consequence in the big picture. Low levels of adrenaline and epinephrine are required for maximizing the positive impact of play on the prefrontal cortex. Keeping the pressure off ensures your brain gets the maximum benefit possible.[7] This means that highly competitive play, like professional sports or gambling when your life savings are on the line, doesn't have the same effect.

- **Be open.** Adopting a playful mindset is all about allowing yourself to expand the number of outcomes that you are willing to entertain. Allow yourself to think outside the box. Indulge your curiosity and step beyond the familiar.

- **Try out new roles.** Be willing to put yourself into an unfamiliar role or position. Psychologists define a role as the collection of expectations that accompanies

---

7. Stephen M. Siviy and Jaak Panksepp, "In Search of the Neurobiological Substrates for Social Playfulness in Mammalian Brains," *Neuroscience & Biobehavioral Reviews* 35, no. 9 (October 2011), https://www.sciencedirect.com/science/article/abs/pii/S0149763411000492?via=ihub.

a particular social position. It is the part you play as a member of a social group, and that identity shapes your behavior.[8] This is true in life as well as during play. If you are normally the leader, be a follower. Shift in and out of character. Allow your brain to take on new roles and adjust the way you interact with the world as a result. Embrace the opportunity to perform new roles and see the world from different perspectives.

- **Look toward laughter.** If there is ever a moment to bring humor to the table, this is it. Humor is healing, and the power of laughter has a long and well-documented legacy. Even the book of Proverbs, in chapter 17, verse 22, alludes to it: "A cheerful heart is good medicine, but a crushed spirit dries up the bones" (NIV). Humor lowers our defenses and stimulates reward centers of the brain.[9] Laughter has also been documented to reduce stress and decrease levels of the stress hormone cortisol.[10] Consider it a brain booster to any intentional play.

---

8. Saul Mcleod, "Social Roles," Simply Psychology, 2008, https://www.simplypsychology.org/social-roles.html.

9. Brandon M. Savage et al., "Humor, Laughter, Learning, and Health! A Brief Review," *Advances in Physiology Education* 41, no. 3 (2017), https://journals.physiology.org/doi/full/10.1152/advan.00030.2017.

10. Dexter Louie et al., "The Laughter Prescription: A Tool for Lifestyle Medicine," *American Journal of Lifestyle Medicine* 10, no. 4 (2016), https://www.ncbi.nlm.nih.gov/pmc/articles/PMC6125057/.

- **Have fun.** Focus not on the outcome of winning, but rather on the joy of the experience. Having fun serves a neurological purpose in the form of a powerful dopamine release. This positively impacts our memory, creativity, motivation, and curiosity. Overall, joy has an important relationship with our propensity to learn and enables many higher cognitive functions.[11]

If you haven't played in a long time or the concept entirely feels uncomfortable and foreign to you, here are some simple ideas for how to incorporate it into your life.

First, ask yourself what you enjoy doing. Create a short list of activities that fit into the broad concept of play. Then think about activities that you have always wanted to do but perhaps have never tried before. Add those to your list.

If you are coming up short on ideas, I have got you covered. Here are over thirty different examples of activities that you can explore as part of adding a dose of play to your everyday life:

- **Creative pursuits:** drawing, painting, sculpture, pottery, photography, knitting, candle making, scrapbooking, doodling (my personal favorite!), calligraphy, cooking, woodworking

---

11. Claire Liu et al., *Neuroscience and Learning through Play: A Review of the Evidence*, LEGO Foundation, November 2017, https://cms.learningthroughplay.com/media /zbcd21td/neuroscience-review_web.pdf.

- **Movement:** recreational sports, dancing, hiking, biking, yoga, hopscotch, creating an obstacle course (a random but potentially game-changing group activity!), paddleboarding
- **Old-fashioned fun:** puzzles, board games, trivia, crosswords, card games, dominos, kite flying, yo-yoing
- **Modern options:** escape rooms, video games, improv (yes, and let me know how it goes!)

Remember when Play-Doh was nothing more than a substance used to take soot off of wallpaper? Not only was the creative thinking of a brilliant nursery school teacher the product's saving grace, but its ability to be used for imaginative play is what propelled it into becoming a household name.

When you live your life in an environment of flexibility, openness, exploration, and creativity, you are able to connect dots that other people cannot see. It is not surprising in the least that a teacher who leveraged play as a tool for learning was able to do what a corporate executive could not: think outside the box.

I was once in a group brainstorming session where we were trying to solve a particularly challenging problem. We were shouting out ideas and drafting them on the whiteboard, and we weren't getting anywhere. Offering up a suggestion on the spot, aloud in front of all of your colleagues, is a bit daunting. It also forces you to vet an idea and run it through that behavioral inhibition system to ensure that it measures up before contributing it to the group. This type of rigid thinking wasn't going to lead to a creative solution.

So to switch it up, we turned the brainstorming into a game.

Each person had five minutes to write down all of their ideas on sticky notes at their desk before sharing with the group. The challenge was to come up with the most ridiculous, improbable idea. Whoever threw out the worst suggestion won. Yes, I said the worst suggestion.

This, as you can imagine, completely transformed the brainstorming session. People started joking with one another, lightly taunting that they were going to have the most ridiculous idea, and the pressure to be "the best" was replaced by a fun, low-stakes opportunity to think outside the box. You were encouraged to look like a fool, and it changed everything.

The ideas that came out of that game were indeed outlandish; however, they were also extraordinarily creative and brave. Many of the concepts, with a slight bit of tweaking and refinement, were actually solid options for solving our dilemma.

The next time you are faced with a challenge or feel stuck and unable to move forward, remove the rigidity of pressure and try to turn it into play. What if thinking outside the box and trying something completely different and unexpected are precisely the things that will propel you forward into greatness?

Give it a shot. Shout out your most ridiculous ideas. See what happens next.

Pattern Interruptions

The definition of insanity is repeating the same process repeatedly and expecting a different result...and yet that is precisely what so many of us do when it comes to allowing the fear of other people's opinions to hold us frozen in fear.

It is like driving off the road into a muddy ditch and simply flooring it over and over again. The wheels keep spinning, the dirt keeps flying, and yet it doesn't matter how many times you hit the gas, you are not going anywhere. You need to get out of the car, find a little friction, and slowly work your way back out.

When we fall into a rut, our mind works precisely the same way. When we find ourselves feeling stuck, we allow our fears to spiral, and no matter how hard we try, we can't make forward progress.

This is where pattern disruption comes in.

The first step in the pattern-disruption process is becoming aware of what your patterns are.

Ask yourself these questions:

- What are the internal narratives that I am repeating to myself? Think back to some of our conversations about insecurities, doubts, and internal soundtracks. When you catch yourself having limiting beliefs or insecurities, write them down to hold yourself accountable for addressing them.

- What are the actions or lack thereof that are keeping me stuck? Keep yourself honest. Think about your current coping mechanisms or ways you perhaps should be caring for yourself that you aren't executing on.

Becoming aware of your thoughts and behavioral patterns is the first step in uncovering how to change them. When you experience the pattern, bring it to your conscious awareness and recognize that you are doing it. This grants you the opportunity to make a change.

Think of these disruptions like tiny pivots. You are heading in one direction and then you spin on your heels to go in another. Pivoting reframes failure from an ending to a new beginning. It builds on your existing momentum and shifts it in the trajectory of something different and hopefully better.

This reminds me of the time that I made a terrible parenting mistake. It was a real rookie mistake too.

I bought a bag of lollipops.

Now, this wasn't just any bag of lollipops. If you have ever done a bulk buy at Costco or Sam's Club, then you know precisely what type of bag I am talking about. I bought the largest bag of lollipops that I had ever seen. Perhaps the largest bag in the world.

It required two hands to lift and was the length of my torso. It was a sugary behemoth—a colossal mountain of every mouthwatering flavor in existence. Why would I do such a thing?

That, my friend, is the million-dollar question. Somewhere between closing my car door and walking into the store, I lost all of my good sense. I forgot that I had a young toddler at home with zero self-control and that we had no need for that many lollipops. I just saw the bag, looked at the great price, and hauled it into the cart.

For the next several days, my toddler was incessantly begging us for lollipops...

Breakfast: "Can I have a lollipop?"

Lunch: "Mommy, lollipop, please?"

Dinner: "No chicken! Lollipop!"

3 a.m.: "Lollipop?"

It was an endless cycle of pleading, persistence, and tantrums as my sweet child's hyperfixation on these sugary little suckers grew. He knew about the gargantuan bag and where it was located, so I did the only rational thing that I could think of.

I wrote a ransom letter from the villain of his favorite cartoon.

"I took your lollipops," the letter said, and it was signed by none other than Mayor Humdinger from *PAW Patrol*.

When my son found the letter, he was equal parts excited and angry. Somehow this cartoon mayor broke into our house in the middle of the night and did that thing that villains do! He stole the world's largest bag of lollipops and disappeared without a trace!

We ran around the house looking for clues, and my son was no longer captivated by the lollipops but instead by finding the fictional thief.

Eventually, my son pleaded with me to call the real PAW Patrol and put the investigative police dog, Chase, on the case. I agreed to try and posted on social media, asking if anyone knew this heroic team of puppies and could inform them of Mayor Humdinger's misdeeds.

Well, the video unexpectedly went viral. Over a million views, thousands of comments, hundreds of shares—the world was determined to see my toddler's dream realized and bring the lollipop thief to justice. The internet did what the internet sometimes does and found the folks at the top (or in this case, the pups at the top), and I received a direct message from the official *PAW Patrol* social media team.

A few days later, a box arrived on our front porch. It was filled to the brim with all sorts of snacks and a letter written from all the pups confirming that Mayor Humdinger had indeed eaten all of the lollipops.

My son's eyes were like saucers, his little voice triumphantly shouting, "Mommy, all the pups sent me this. They are real. The pups are real!" To my toddler, this was the greatest moment in his three short years of life.

That's the power of pattern interruption with a dose of improvisation.

I made a mistake and it caused a negative pattern to arise. The begging, crying, and nonstop tantrums were making my son and me miserable. Instead of repeating the same cycle over and over again, I redirected his attention elsewhere.

Did I make up an absolutely ridiculous story about a fictional villain running off into the sunset with the bag of lollipops? Embarrassing as it is to admit, yes I did.

Did it work and was it worth it? One hundred percent yes!

Imagine if Kutol Products simply continued repeating the same sales and marketing strategies for its wallpaper cleaner, knowing that demand was decreasing. The product would eventually have died a slow and unremarkable death.

By pivoting instead, Play-Doh became the household name that so many families love (and others curse repeatedly under their breath while vacuuming dried dough off the floor for the one thousandth time).

Having the courage to pivot sometimes reveals new opportunities that exist and talents that we didn't even know we had. How often have you looked back on your life and seen those big pivotal moments and realized that you found something you weren't even looking for?

You set out to do one thing, pivoted, pivoted again, and before you knew it, you landed precisely where you were always meant to be. When we are open to the possibilities of what could be, we create space for opportunity and leave ourselves open to the power of the pivot.

CHAPTER 10

RISKY BUSINESS

There's something I am really drawn to about risk. I love the moment of standing on the edge of a cliff and just jumping. I have always been drawn to that feeling, to that moment, and I am not afraid of it.
—JEREMY COWART

I had the opportunity to interview someone I deeply admire in the process of writing this book. A creative who has dedicated over fifteen years of his life to pushing the bounds of photography and creating art that captivates. Someone who made me realize that it is possible to take massive risks and carve out your own path. His name is Jeremy Cowart.

Jeremy is a renowned photographer and respected artist who specializes in celebrity portraiture and humanitarian photography projects around the world.

I could sit here and make a list of all of the inspiring people that he has had in front of his camera—names like Sting,

Emma Stone, Taylor Swift, Tyler Perry, Brandi Carlile, Britney Spears, Barack Obama, and so many others—but that isn't why I admire him.

It isn't who he has worked with that is most impressive. It isn't the scale of his business or the countless accolades that he has received. It isn't the national movement he started to encourage creatives to give back, or the massive NFT collection he dropped that sold out within seconds—it isn't even the fact that every time I play Lauren Daigle's music on Spotify, I see his photograph on the album cover.

The thing that inspires me most about Jeremy Cowart is his boundless courage. It is the way that he takes risks artistically, the way he leaps genres entirely, the way he uses his creativity to make an impact in ways that no one else thought to do. He isn't following a career path or even "taking the road less traveled"—he is on his own journey entirely.

When we talked about how he navigates the fear of what other people think, he jumped into a story about a retreat that he went to as a kid. Jeremy vividly remembers standing at the base of a daunting ropes course that extended thirty feet up into the air. The instructor looked around at the assembled group and asked, "Who wants to go first?"

Jeremy's hand shot up. Without hesitation, without any inkling of indecision, he threw his hat into the ring. When he looked around, he saw that he was the only one out of the entire group who had put up his hand. No one else wanted to do it. Not a single person other than him wanted to go first.

That really stuck with him.

If you have ever wondered what the impact of a life of radical curiosity is, this is it. Jeremy's story reminded me that every day, we are one raised hand away from an entirely different life.

When we feel that flicker of interest or that desire placed upon our heart to leap, it is up to us to rise to the occasion. No one else can live your life for you, so stop giving people's opinions permission to hold you back.

Take a risk. Raise your hand.

Discover what awaits you when you live with boundless courage.[1, 2]

Risky Business

I have learned a lot from being around entrepreneurial people. Since I was eighteen years old, I have run one kind of business or another. Most of my closest friends are either entrepreneurs themselves or they are married to one. I eat, sleep, and breathe small business.

So, trust me when I say that entrepreneurial people are wired a little differently. I don't know whether we are born this way or if we stumble into it accidentally, but I have always been curious about what it is that makes us tick.

1. Ryan Essmaker and Tina Essmaker, "Jeremy Cowart," *The Great Discontent,* March 12, 2013, https://thegreatdiscontent.com/interview/jeremy-cowart/.
2. Jeremy Cowart, interview by the author, July 22, 2022.

In nearly every definition of "entrepreneurship" that you can find, you will see this one word used. Regardless of whether it is referencing the people who lead large ventures or small entities, it pops up over and over again.

The word is "risk."

To be an entrepreneur means to take a risk—or, more accurately, infinite micro-risks accumulating in a larger endeavor that is ultimately a risk in and of itself.

When you choose to take a risk, it means that you knowingly expose yourself to the potential of an adverse outcome. If things don't work out, there will be a cost. The magnitude of that cost varies, but the underlying mindset at play is often the same.

Risk-taking isn't limited to entrepreneurship. There are always some individuals who are more apt to seek out precarious or high-pressure roles in different aspects of their lives. Firefighters, military personnel, emergency medical professionals—anyone who chooses to run into a burning building or rescue someone in a moment of crisis certainly fits the bill.

On a lighter note, think about all of the people playing sports who raise their hand and agree to be the goalie. Bear with me here...Goalies are certainly unique human beings.

They consciously choose to have a ball or puck catapulted directly at their head at an intense rate of speed...over and over again.

Oh, and just in case you aren't familiar with what goalies do, their job isn't to get out of the way of the rapidly speeding object. Oh no, not one bit! They have to use a random body part or a stick of some kind to stop the flying projectile before it makes contact with the net.

If they succeed at stopping the ball or puck, it is the highest of highs.

If they fail, the weight of the loss comes down directly onto their shoulders.

Whew! I know what you are thinking...Why on earth would anyone choose to be the goalie? Why would someone choose to put themselves in a high-stakes and potentially dangerous position when they could choose to cheer safely from the stands?

I didn't know the answer myself, so I decided to call my sister.

You see, my younger sister, Caroline, is one of those people. She played lacrosse. Of all the positions that she could have chosen to be growing up, she decided to be the goalie. It turns out that she was extremely good at it too. She played competitively all throughout middle and high school and ended up playing lacrosse all four years at Princeton.

What was her answer as to why she chose that position? "I loved the adrenaline. You are the final line of defense. It comes down to you and the ball. That's it."

I wish you could have heard the exhilaration and passion in her voice as she talked about this experience with me. It was as if she truly came alive thinking back to all those years she spent in the goal.

A lot of us have felt that same spark. It is the little bit of electricity that ignites within our soul when we do what we love and take the risks that matter.

Entrepreneurship or athleticism is just a means to express that very human desire to step into the arena, set aside what is comfortable and familiar, and go for it.

Taking a risk is the ultimate act of hope.

How we choose to take risks may look different for all of us, but the underlying way it makes us feel is universal...alive! It makes us feel alive.

Risk-Taking 101

Let's talk about some simple ways to get better at taking risks. Being a small-business owner has taught me a lot when it comes to discerning the good opportunities from the bad ones and how to mitigate risks to improve the likelihood of positive outcomes.

Here are a few of my biggest tips:

- **Break it down.** When you are deciding whether to go for something risky, break the larger risk into incremental pieces. Starting with smaller risks can build your confidence in taking larger risks. It also can inform your overall strategy and increase your likelihood of success. For example, if you want to become a published author but the thought of writing an entire book is too daunting, consider starting a blog and committing to writing one post per week. If you want to start a small business but aren't able to leave your full-time job and assume such a large financial risk, consider starting a side hustle.

- **Weigh the costs and benefits.** Think about what you're gaining versus what you would be giving up if you took a particular risk. Be clear about the costs and benefits of any given outcome and use it to weigh your options. If you were able to break your risks down into smaller potential risks, this is also a great place to compare and contrast different options for how you may want to move forward. Seeing the bigger picture may provide clarity on the best route to take.

- **Mitigate your threats.** Risk mitigation is a common strategy used to prepare for threats and lessen the possibility of failure. At its very core, this simply means identifying, assessing, and controlling risks by taking an intentional approach to decrease threats from the outset. Consider asking yourself, What is my risk tolerance? What are the potential ways this could go wrong? What could be done to lessen the likelihood of adverse outcomes? This is a very simplified version, but the key point is to be thoughtful and find ways to reduce the possibility of negative outcomes.

- **Create a safety net.** Especially for risks that pose a significant threat to something like your stability or finances, having a safety net is critically important. This is one of the biggest pieces of advice that I give to business owners who want to quit a corporate job and become a full-time independent. Build up your financial runway to ensure that you can continue operating and paying yourself for a significant amount of time in the event that it takes a while to ramp up your income. Safety nets come in all shapes and sizes. When there are not tight timelines around potential risks and you have the luxury of planning in advance, incorporate building a safety net into your overall execution plan.

- **Be honest about failure.** When evaluating a risk, it is important to be honest with yourself about what failure would mean for you and for those who you are responsible for. This isn't meant to deter you or make risk-taking scarier. Instead, it is important to ensure before you take the leap that you could weather the fallout if things go wrong.

- **Give yourself permission to quit.** I absolutely detest the saying "Winners never quit" because the most successful entrepreneurs that I know have started and quit many different things until they found what worked best for them. When you enter into a risk knowing that you can quit at any time, it reduces the pressure. It also allows you to approach risk-taking more playfully, which we know rewires the brain and can lead to better outcomes.

The Cost of Settling

Sometimes we become so focused on the potential consequences of taking a risk that we forget that there are also repercussions when we settle for less than we desire or deserve. That comes with its own challenges too.

When facing two paths, one that is certain and the other that is an unknown, ask yourself, What would I regret more—taking this risk and it not working out or staying the course and spending the rest of my life wondering what could have been?

This simple reframe shifts the weight of uncertainty from the risk and places it on the potential regret of never having taken that chance. It chooses failure as the outcome of the unknown path, thereby also ensuring that you confront the worst-case scenario before choosing to leap.

Sometimes shifting our perspective to view decisions through a retrospective lens gives us the clarity we need to make a better choice in the moment.

It also reminds us that holding on and choosing the path of continuation has consequences. Humans, being pain avoidant and risk averse, often forget that fact. We see continuity and familiarity as less likely to cause us harm than the unknown... even when that isn't the case.

Staying safely within the bounds of your comfort zone or settling for the familiar may not feel like a risk until you view it through a retrospective lens. How will you feel about this choice far into the future? What is the impact of not taking a particular risk when you zoom out several decades?

There isn't a perfect response to this question. For some, failure is not an option, or they are not in a position where taking the riskier path is a possibility. For others, failure would be a survivable reality...a painful one, but one that would still be better than the alternative.

What's important to remember is that any decision in life will have consequences, but only you can decide which path to take forward. Other people will have opinions or make judgments, but they aren't the one living your life—you are.

Suck at Something If You Want To

Have you ever heard the phrase "a Jack of all trades is a master of none"? I am fairly certain there isn't a person reading this book who hasn't come across the illustrious saying.

I was surprised to find out recently that the quote we have all come to associate with niching down or becoming an expert or staying in our lane isn't, in fact, about that at all. There is a second part to the quote that was somehow lost along the road to popularity, and it fundamentally transforms the meaning.

The entire saying goes like this:

"A jack of all trades is a master of none, but oftentimes better than a master of one."

In other words, oftentimes you are better off trying a multitude of different things, even if you don't end up mastering any particular one of them. Now that, my friends, is a bit of advice that I can truly get behind.

I have always felt like growing up is similar to walking down a giant funnel. At the start, your life is wide open and then gets narrower and narrower the farther you go along.

When you are little, there is this multitude of possibilities around you, and you are often encouraged to try everything. However, as you get older and you begin to move deeper and deeper into that funnel, you are required to choose.

Will you go to college? What will you study? What field will you choose to pursue? What occupation will you go into within that field? What specialty will you take? Narrower and narrower we go.

You want specialization in a cardiothoracic surgeon when they are operating on your heart or an aeronautical engineer when they are launching rockets into space, but that shouldn't mean that even the experts have to stop exploring new possibilities. Growing up shouldn't mean having to surrender the part of ourselves that dreams, wonders, explores, and tinkers with new things. Low-stakes opportunities give you a safe space to take risks and explore.

When it comes to taking risks, we have a tendency to limit ourselves by believing that we must stay in our lane. If you are a teacher, you should teach. If you are a marketer, you should market. I could go on and on.

The opinions of others have a tendency to keep pushing you down that funnel of who you should be without allowing you to expand the possibilities of who you could become. There is a place in this world for the multifaceted and multipassionate parts of you. There are new interests awaiting you and new opportunities around every corner.

What if you didn't stay in your lane?

What if instead of believing that it was too late, you chose to bet on you? What if instead of believing that you missed your shot, you went after it today? What if instead of feeling drained by the monotony of life, you did something radically spontaneous?

Everyone loves to say that life is short—myself included.

However, do you know what life also is? Long. Yep, life is freaking long.

Or at least life has a much longer runway than we often realize. We often tell ourselves that it is too late or too difficult or not possible for us without even exploring what it would look like to make a change or take a risk or explore a possibility.

Is there a chance that it might not happen for you? Certainly. However, it is a guarantee that it won't if you never open your mind to the opportunity in the first place.

If you want to pick up a new hobby at sixty, do it. If you are in your thirties and you want to pivot careers, do it. If you have always wanted to start a blog or get on TikTok or take an improv class, do it.

You don't have to be the best. Heck, you don't even have to be good.

I think that we forget that little fact when we talk about things like taking risks and being courageous. It is often confined to such a professional context that we lose sight of the fact that it doesn't always mean doing something in a high-pressure scenario. Some of the best risks that we ever take in our lives are small and spontaneous.

In those situations, you have the freedom to be absolutely terrible.

Yes, I really just said that. Be absolutely terrible. Make a fool of yourself.

Sucking at something you love is still better than not doing it at all. Perhaps being bad at something you love is even better than being great at something that truly makes you miserable.

Who cares if people don't understand why you are doing it? Who cares if they tease or judge you? Remember: they are going to have opinions about you either way.

So for goodness' sake—if they are going to criticize you, at least let it be for going after what you want. When the stakes are low and you aren't facing a matter of life and death, why not go for it?

Get out there and suck if you want to...

Be the worst painter in the entire world. Do a cringey dance on TikTok. Write a book that never sells a copy. Run a race and come in last. Knit a scarf no one will ever wear. Launch a blog with your mom as the only reader. Make a soufflé that no one wants to eat. Sing karaoke and get booed off stage.

Go after what you want and fail miserably in the pursuit of it. Why the heck not? As long as it doesn't cause actual harm to you or anyone else (thankfully death by embarrassment isn't possible, as far as I am aware), go for it. If the fear of being bad at something is what is holding you back, I sure hope this gives you the permission you need to move forward.

Friend, you don't get another shot at living today. It is a one-and-done kind of deal. So go after what you want, try something new, and don't be afraid to suck.

How would your life be different if instead of only doing the things you're good at or that you are familiar with, you committed to spending one year trying all of the things you suspect you would be terrible at?

Think of it like 365 days of doing things you suck at.

Make a list of the activities you have failed at in the past or things you never learned how to do as a kid that you've avoided in adulthood for fear of looking stupid. Add in some bucket-list items that just seem ridiculous to try. Even throw in the tiny, insignificant things that you wish you were better at.

Learning to do your own makeup. Going Rollerblading. Learning choreography to a popular song. Apologizing. I could keep going...

What if you looked for opportunities to do the very things

you sucked at? How do you imagine your life might look? What do you think that level of freedom might feel like?

And what kind of permission do you feel that might even give to those around you...especially those who look up to you? Imagine if you had always felt safe to try new things and come in last place. What a very different world this might be.

CHAPTER 11

MAKING A FOOL OF YOURSELF

I remember the day I frantically typed, "Is Mercury in retrograde and what the heck does that even mean?" into Google. It is that thing that people love to say, and while I still don't understand it entirely, I do know this...Sometimes it feels like our lives are a downright dumpster fire.

I was having one of those weeks. In the span of a few days, I made a fool of myself repeatedly and publicly...over and over again. It was almost comical.

I started by face-planting in the Indianapolis airport while running to catch a flight—sprawled out like a starfish, coffee cup flying through the air like a dangerously hot projectile, while onlookers gawked as the sound of my body went *thump* on the hard linoleum floor.

What made it worse is that people didn't even stop. They just continued stepping around me, rushing off to catch their flights. I lay there on the floor for a few seconds, completely in shock, as the world rushed on around me. It was mortifying.

Then over the next few days, the ridiculousness continued. I gave a talk with food in my teeth, sent a text message to someone I admire where autocorrect fundamentally made me sound like a weirdo, and showed up to a networking event with dog poop on my shoes.

Yes—dog poop.

To be honest, I thought that the person I was talking to just smelled bad without realizing the entire time that it was, in fact, me who stunk to high heaven. Obviously, I didn't say anything. Then again, no one said anything to me either. It's funny how we avoid awkwardness in that way. Preferring to continue on as if nothing is wrong rather than risking embarrassing ourselves or others.

Imagine my surprise when I came home and I finally figured it out when the stink followed me all the way back. I was horrified. I couldn't believe that I had walked around a room full of people I respect for over an hour smelling like...well, you know...poop.

Don't Take Yourself Too Seriously

You are going to, at some point, make a complete fool of yourself. It might be once in a blue moon or six times in the span of a week, but it will eventually happen.

There is no avoiding it. Embarrassing mistakes and mishaps are inevitable. Nowadays, with the rapid pace of life and the fact that everything is shared by everyone online and our brains are constantly running on empty, it is a miracle that we don't embarrass ourselves more often.

Forgetting to hit mute in a big Zoom meeting.

Giving a big talk with your zipper down.

Making a good old-fashioned Freudian slip.

Walking around with spit-up on your shirt.

Saying "I love you" at the end of a work call.

How on earth do we keep moving forward when we are all one second away from becoming the next internet meme? Okay, that one is a joke. What I really mean to say is…

How do we find the courage to try new things knowing that we're just one misstep away from making a fool of ourselves? How do we embrace the fact that we will at some point feel embarrassed or will do something that other people think is ridiculous?

As we get older and the expectations we place upon ourselves get higher, it creates a narrative that to look foolish in the eyes of others is a fate worse than death. We avoid humiliation at all costs, even when it keeps us from going after what we want in life.

This manifests a little differently for everyone. It can mean avoiding potential rejection, like failing to ask for what we deserve, go after our dreams, or even imagine something bigger for our lives. It can mean failing to put ourselves out there, like hiding from the spotlight or public view whenever possible. Sometimes it means shrinking back, diminishing our light, and doing everything that we can to go unnoticed.

It is akin to fear of failure, and yet the fear of looking foolish in the eyes of others holds many of us back far more than we realize. Embarrassment is a neighbor of shame and guilt.[1] It is where the opinions of those around us are weaponized against us by our own doing. They become like handcuffs keeping us from reaching for what we want in life. But here's the thing...

Gutsy living means having the courage to make a fool of yourself.

---

1. J. P. Tangney et al., "Are Shame, Guilt, and Embarrassment Distinct Emotions?," *Journal of Personality and Social Psychology* 70, no. 6 (1996): 1256–1269, https://doi.org/10.1037/0022-3514.70.6.1256.

It means raising your hand, using your voice, and sometimes even stepping into the spotlight—knowing all the while that sometimes we will make mistakes, mess up, or earn the laughter of the crowd. It means learning not to take yourself too seriously, to accept that failure is a part of life and mistakes are bound to happen.

We have to learn to lighten up. Laugh a little. Embrace the fact that someday we are going to be the butt of the joke or the one to face-plant in an airport. Someday we are going to go after a big dream and fail miserably...publicly...and people will notice.

As uncomfortable as that may be, hiding from embarrassment won't ever make it go away. We have to step right up to it and give it a giant bear hug. We have to invite it to the party as an honored guest and recognize that it isn't so scary after all.

The best antidote to embarrassment is humility and vulnerability. You have to embrace it. Acknowledge that it exists and be honest about the fact that it doesn't feel all that great.

When we don't create space for our feelings of embarrassment, they can take root and become something a bit darker and more damaging. They can take a deeper hold on us and keep us from taking risks or trusting ourselves in the future.

Holding on to the discomfort or running through scenarios over and over again in your mind after you make a fool of yourself won't change what happened. It will only keep you trapped and unable to move forward.

When I was learning how to do free throws in high school

basketball, I struggled with missing the rim. I was terrified of shooting an airball, and somehow the fear of doing it almost held me back from continuing to play the game. It wasn't until I actually did airball midgame with a packed auditorium that I realized something incredibly important...It didn't kill me.

So I did it again. Not intentionally, of course, but later on that game it happened a second time, and I found that I felt less embarrassment than when it happened before. The more I failed, the less I feared failing. The more mortified I felt, the less it seemed to bother me the next time.

Imagine for a moment that I gave you an assignment—to go out into the world and risk embarrassing yourself once every day. What if you made a point of jumping into ridiculous situations and immersing yourself in the very fear that is holding you back?

Sing an unpopular song at the top of your lungs with your windows down in the car.

Wear your shirt backward and walk around in public until someone lets you know.

Start a meeting by reciting a poem and give zero explanation whatsoever.

Put on an over-the-top costume for a friend's birthday...when that isn't the theme.

Hold a sign on a street corner that says, "Honk if you like pineapple on pizza."

I could keep going, but I think you can visualize how you might feel in any of those given scenarios. Mortified? Ridiculous? Uncomfortable? Probably all of the above, and that is to be expected.

However, if you had to do them and had absolutely zero choice in the matter, what do you think would be the outcome? Think about it. None of the aforementioned scenarios would kill you. I am willing to bet that with each progressing act of embarrassment, you would start to feel a little more confident in your ability to handle it. You might even begin to view embarrassment through the lens of opportunity.

Instead of being engulfed in negative emotions, you might even be able to see lessons and wisdom in those experiences. Dare I say that you might even have a little more fun with the assignment along the way—learning to love the freedom that comes from living with less rigidity and fear over what others may think.

This is precisely what Jia Jiang did one decade ago.

He spent one hundred days going out of his way to be rejected by others in order to overcome the very thing that he knew was holding him back. One rejection per day. He walked into a FedEx and asked to mail a box to Santa Claus. He attempted to make an announcement on a Southwest flight. He tried to get a haircut from a dog groomer at PetSmart.

The outcome? He became more comfortable getting rejected and gained surprising insights along the way.

When he started asking people who rejected him why they chose to say no, he discovered their answers had more to do with themselves than they had to do with him. This is parallel to the understanding that many of the fears that we have racing around in our head are often worse than the reality of how someone else feels about us. We tend to be our own harshest critics.

Likewise, when people were encouraged to acknowledge how weird his requests were, it increased the likelihood of that rejection turning into a yes. As if the awkwardness of the situation created a sense of connection and trust that wasn't there before.[2]

Whether it is fear of rejection or fear of embarrassment, remember that there is power in being able to move toward something without letting your fear get in the way. As the saying goes, nothing ventured, nothing gained. Exposing yourself to the very thing you are afraid of, especially in safe, low-stakes situations, can give you the confidence to push forward.

Just like putting one foot in front of the other, you can slowly feel more comfortable in situations that may have embarrassed you or made you feel anxious in the past. By taking steps in the direction of your fear and little by little making

---

2. Jia Jiang, *Rejection Proof: How to Beat Fear and Become Invincible* (New York: Random House, 2016).

it less of an intimidating threat, you will uncover that you are able to handle far more than you ever thought possible.

While this doesn't require you to stand on a street corner asking people if they like pineapple on their pizza—which is an unexpectedly controversial question, I might add—that might not be the worst way to jump into the deep end. If you end up doing it, be sure to let me know.

Getting Comfortable with the Uncomfortable

Several years ago, I chose "fearless" as my word of the year, and I made a commitment to say yes to anything that I wanted to do but in the past had been too afraid to attempt. This goal had me signing up to do all sorts of wild things—most notably, I got a tattoo and went bungee jumping on the same day.

I may have taken my word of the year a little bit too seriously...However, it certainly proved to be a successful strategy to get out of my comfort zone. Realistically, this type of exposure strategy isn't for everyone.

There are other very simple ways to expand your tolerance for navigating embarrassing situations and the fear of other people's opinions.

Own up to how you're feeling: *Embrace the sensation and be open about it. Whether the situation is your fault or not, simply pointing out how* *embarrassed you feel can create feelings of connection and intimacy with those around you and help other people to feel more comfortable too. Shared experiences build empathy, and often one of the best things you can do is let others in on your emotion in a humble and gracious way.*

Practice vulnerability: *Being vulnerable about how something makes you feel is a compelling force for navigating difficult situations. When we make a fool of ourselves or feel embarrassed about something, there is power in being able to address the situation without veering from the pain of it all or trying to downplay our emotions. Even if you are unable to address the situation head-on in the moment, having other people that you can be open and vulnerable with around you will help you to navigate your emotions and access community support.*

Know that you are your own worst critic: *Remind yourself that you are judging yourself more harshly than anyone else is—no one else is running through all the mistakes you made in their mind before falling asleep. Right? They are likely doing that to themselves. We are generally our own harshest critics, and we have a tendency to criticize ourselves more harshly than other people do.*

Attention is short; focus is fleeting: *One of my favorite quotes in the world is from the show* Ted Lasso: *"You know what the happiest animal on earth is? It's a goldfish. It's got a ten-second memory."*[3] *The truth is that people will forget your embarrassing moments just as quickly as they happened in the first place. Our attention spans are short, and our focus is fleeting. The interesting thing is that for most people, their memory about your minor mishaps disappears almost instantly. While you may cling to that moment and relive the embarrassment over and over again, no one else does. Remember that.*

More Than a Misstep

What about when your mistake is more than a misstep? What about the times when embarrassment or deeper feelings of shame creep in because the stakes were high and the world was watching?

Face-planting in the airport was a minor moment of embarrassment compared to some of the larger failures that I have experienced in my life. Business ventures that crumbled, partnerships that didn't pan out...I even once launched a podcast that lasted two whole weeks. Yep, that's it. Two weeks after a

---

3. *Ted Lasso*, Season 1, Episode 2, "Biscuits." 2020, Apple TV+.

very public launch. I felt like a complete fool to put something out into the world and then have it stop so soon afterward.

I shared my infertility journey for years, including several cycles that failed and the sting that came with each passing month of negative tests. I think those failures were perhaps the hardest to navigate with the world watching.

I have no doubt that more moments precisely like these await me in the years to come. I may be an optimist at heart, but I know that I will once again go after what I want in life and fall short of the outcome that I desire. That is how things go.

Failure—it's not a great feeling, is it?

Especially when it is something that you deeply wanted or hoped would work out and it doesn't. It hurts to watch your dreams go up in flames and catch the attention of every-one around you. It is as if the smoke keeps billowing upward in a giant signal indicating, "Look over here! My life is fall-ing apart," as it grabs the attention of anyone and everyone for miles.

With the world watching and how public our lives have become, there seems to be a new level of embarrassment that we are forced to experience these days when things fall apart. I am talking about the type of failure that leaves your stomach in knots and your heart aching.

The relationship that didn't work out...and the countless publicly shared photographs and digital reminders that sur-round you. It is the switch of a status back to single and the pain you must experience as that person continues on with their life publicly too.

The layoff from the dream job you were so excited about... You find yourself getting a pink slip and having to update everyone that you are now unemployed, and you feel like a fool for thinking it would be the next step in your career.

The loss of anything or anyone who you thought would be a part of your future. The chances you took hoping it would pan out that failed painfully. The decisions you made or words you said that you wish you could take back. We will experience hard things and rarely will we endure it without the eyes of others watching. That is the world that we now live in.

As a result, it is natural to struggle with negative emotions at the hands of others' opinions in our lives. With our worlds being shared in snippets and updates on the internet, our successes are celebrated by a wider group of people; however, our failures are more publicly observed as well. The increased awareness and added eyes on our every loss and setback can feel overwhelming. Frankly, sometimes it even becomes incapacitating.

Experiencing hardship and being forced to simultaneously navigate external opinions and feedback can keep you from wanting to share your life with others at all. It can also keep you from going after the very things that you desire most.

When you feel the razor-sharp sting of shame piercing you from the inside, you will do anything to avoid feeling that again. I know that all too well. Perhaps part of the reason that you picked up this book is because you have felt it too.

Often when we are afraid of what other people think of us, it isn't because of some lofty hypothetical scenario that holds us back...It is the emotional pain that lingers from past suffering.

We are not always running away from the things that scare us about the future. Sometimes we are trying to outrun a past that feels too painful to process. Sometimes we are doing whatever we can to avoid enduring that feeling once again.

The problem is that the only way to truly evade heartache is to not go after anything at all—to avoid any relationship that could hurt us, to push away good opportunities that may not pan out, and to retreat from sharing our life with others in meaningful ways.

Avoiding the pain of future failure will only lead to the greater loss of a life unlived.

That is precisely what we are here to prevent.

That is exactly what inspired me to write this book in the first place.

CHAPTER 12

REWRITE THE RULES

What if you threw the unspoken rule book out the window? What if instead of trying to win at someone else's game, you decided to create your own? New rules. New measurements of success. No more going with the flow and trying to fit into everyone else's expectations of you.

Are you curious what you would uncover? Here's what I know to be true.

The world is not built for the gutsy ones, but it is the gutsy ones who go on to change the world.

No one gets judged too harshly for staying in the shadows. No one is criticized too brutally for keeping their head down, minimizing their accomplishments, and staying on the pre-determined path. Keeping silent and staying stuck certainly won't win you a gold medal, but they sure feel a lot safer... don't they?

There is a cost that comes with getting gutsy. This is a reality that you know all too well.

There is a price that you pay for stepping out into the light. A price that is demanded of you for simply existing as a human who believes they are deserving of more. And that price is most often demanded by people who do not even know you or encouraged by forces that do not desire to see you rise.

Personal attacks. Judgmental dismissals. False perceptions. Gossip spread. Wounding words. Estranged relationships. Rejection.

So we shrink back and choose the comfort of invisibility instead. We do as we are told, we follow the rules, and we color inside the lines. We don't dare rock the boat or make waves. We hope that by playing small we will be spared harm—free from the judgmental spectators and the personal attacks. We hope we will be protected from the criticism, the hateful rhetoric, or the words that jab at our insecurities.

However, at one point or another we realize that no matter how hard we try to minimize ourselves, no matter how small we make our ambitions seem, no matter how much we try to squeeze and shrink and lessen and wither, we are still not small enough.

The opposite is true too. No matter how hard we strive,

how far we climb, or how much we accomplish, we are still not doing enough. We are still somehow failing. We are still falling short. We are reminded at every turn that there is always more that we could be doing.

Never have I felt this more acutely than when I became a mom.

The world expected me to work as if I had no children back at home and raise my babies as if I had no job filling up my working hours. I was told to cover up while breastfeeding and then reminded that "breast is best" when I could not find formula for my daughter months later. I was expected to excel at my career, always go the extra mile, but never at the expense of my mental health or family commitments.

I struggled to cram fifty hours' worth of responsibilities into a single day but feared ever talking about it because hustle culture is toxic. I was told to spend less time on social media but never lose touch with friends. I was encouraged to live my best life but simultaneously shamed for finding joy in hard seasons.

Have you experienced any of this yourself?

Tell me if any of this feels familiar:

Love your body but not too much as to seem vain. Be humble but not so humble that you fail to acknowledge your own accomplishments. Take care of yourself, but don't be selfish. Achieve great things, but don't outshine others. Market your skills and strengths but not too much as to seem egotistical. Put others first, but also make sure not to put yourself last.

You are always too much and not enough at the same time. You are always doing too little and are simultaneously overworked, overwhelmed, and underpaid. There is no space for you, and yet you didn't try hard enough if you didn't claim your seat at the table.

There is no winning at a game that is set up to see you fail.

It is like running on an endless hamster wheel toward a destination that does not exist. It is like navigating an infinite maze that has no exit. This game is not designed to give you what you are looking for. It can't. It won't. It never will.

So what if instead you decided to stop playing? What if you chose to tune out the idea of what others think you should be and instead embrace who you truly are? What if you dared to determine success on your own terms?

Or what if you decided that there was nothing about you that needed fixing at all? Imagine that. What if you stopped trying to change yourself long enough to realize that you are not what is broken after all? Daring words from a self-help writer, and yet… perhaps the most honest thing I have written in this entire book.

What if the world and its expectations are what's broken? Like shoving a square peg in a round hole, what if you have been trying to fit into definitions of success that were never made for you? There are many of you reading this who have spent your entire life feeling like you were not enough. I hope now you are uncovering that the measurement of "enoughness" you have been told to strive for was one you could never achieve. Perhaps because it never existed.

Something profound changes when you realize that you cannot win by the rules of this world. Something shifts when you begin to see that you have been chasing after a finish line that does not exist or that you have been striving for a worthiness that others can never give you.

It is impossible to win a game that is built on contradicting prerequisites for success. You can hold all the pieces in your hand and yet...you will never be enough to declare yourself the victor. You will always be one step behind or falling one position short. You can check every box and succeed at every challenge and yet still never be enough.

At the 2021 Olympics, gymnastics front-runner Simone Biles shocked the world when she pulled out of the women's team final. After a risky vaulting routine made it apparent to her that she was not in the right headspace to compete, she withdrew.

"Put mental health first...." she said. "It's OK sometimes to even sit out the big competitions to focus on yourself, because it shows how strong of a competitor and person that you really are—rather than just battle through it."[4]

At the height of her career, with the world watching, under the weight of everyone's opinions, she made a choice. She chose to put her mental health above what others expected from her. She took a painful and public step back from the very thing she

---

4. Bill Chappell, "Read What Simone Biles Said after Her Withdrawal from the Olympic Final," NPR, July 28, 2021, https://www.npr.org/sections/tokyo-olympics-live-updates /2021/07/28/1021683296/in-her-words-what-simone-biles-said-after-her-withdrawal.

had spent her lifetime working toward because in her heart she decided that it was the right thing.

The cost was brutal: an onslaught of internet hatred, public criticism, and having to watch from the sidelines while others competed at the events that she loved doing most. Making the decision was hard enough; remaining in the public eye in the aftermath was perhaps even tougher.

However, Simone Biles didn't leave the arena. She didn't allow the judgments and insults to break her. She took her place on the sidelines and cheered for every single one of her teammates as they took second place and won the silver medal.

There are a multitude of opinions that exist regarding the choice that Simone Biles made; however, the opinion that matters the most is her own. Pundits and critics will say what they want, but let us not forget that most have never set foot inside that arena—their judgment is cast from the quiet comfort of their office chairs and keyboards.

However, if you ask me, I believe that she exhibited the type of bold, brave, and boundless courage that this book is all about. Why? For having the courage to make a hard choice, for living by her values when the criticism came, by continuing onward with conviction, and for putting her health first in a space where that is so rarely done.

Simone Biles plays by her own rules...and in doing so, she gives countless others the courage to do the same. That is what it means to be gutsy.

Out with the Old, In with the New

"You're so good at what you do. Thank you," she said.

"Oh, it's nothing," I said, shrugging. The words felt so familiar on my tongue—too familiar. How many times had I said that before? A hundred times? A thousand times? Maybe more.

How many times had I downplayed my achievements, avoided praise, or deflected gratitude because it was what I saw so many other "good" women do? How many times have you?

Shortly thereafter, I realized that my concept of what it meant to be "good" was skewed and shaped by the very forces that I so often found myself rebelling against. It was as if someone handed me a definition through subtle cues and years of conditioning and I never once questioned it.

Cultural conditioning slowly envelops us layer by layer, day by day. Slowly, we become buried deep beneath the weight of other people's opinions, worldly expectations, and inaccurate conclusions. We accept societal norms falsely masquerading as absolute truth. It is a delicate dance of praise and punishment that conditions us, adding more layers to the heap without us ever realizing it.

So what happens when you have the courage to peel back the layers? What happens when you realize that being good does not, in fact, require you to make yourself smaller? It is not the byproduct of living in the shadows of someone else's success or hiding from the talents you have been given. It is not earned through your appearance or by pleasing others. It is not enhanced by being amenable or increased by avoiding confrontation.

Frankly, I am no longer chasing after what it means to be "good" anymore. I stopped trying a long time ago. The moment I realized that I valued integrity far more than I valued being perceived as "good" in the eyes of the world, some of those layers of conditioning began to fracture. If being honest and having integrity is what matters more than holding approval in the eyes of others, we must have the courage to seek the truth and fight for it once we find it.

So what is that truth? What are the new rules that we must write to replace the outdated expectations of who we should be?

You are the author of your story. You have listed your values. You have crafted your trusted inner circle. You have unpacked the power of opinions and learned techniques to open your mind. You're ready to take risks and even look like a fool if that is required of you. Now you are ready to rewrite the rules.

What Will Your Rules Be?

If you sat down to write out ten rules to live by, what would you choose? Here are a few to get your mind revving and the inspiration flowing. These are in no particular order.

Honor Your Needs

Remember that choosing to nurture, respect, and honor yourself is not selfish. Ensuring that your own needs are met is not greedy. Spending time getting to know yourself is not egotistical. You deserve to flourish. Don't let the expectations of the world keep you from taking care of yourself. You must ensure your needs are met before you can support anyone else.

Put your hand on your chest, take a deep breath, and ask yourself, What is it that I need today? What does my body need to feel its best? What does my mind need to feel its best? Make a habit of honoring your needs every day. What you choose to water grows. Make sure you are watering the right things and tending to the habits that will enable you to flourish.

Have an Opinion

People are entitled to their opinions and so are you. Have an opinion. Take a point of view. Speak from the heart. Stand up for what is right. Make noise that matters...even if your voice shakes. Have the courage to be disliked for what you believe. Do not surrender your voice in the pursuit of making others love you. Rise from the shadows of hiding and be seen.

Love Your Neighbor

Meet people with empathy and welcome them with open arms. Listen when they share their lived experiences. Be radically inclusive. Remember that we are all neighbors on this small rock floating in the infinite expanse of space. Love is a verb; it requires action. It is not passively sitting by and accepting the status quo but rather is gutsy about building a better future for all. Love your elderly neighbor, your disabled neighbor, your BIPOC neighbor, your LGBTQ+ neighbor. Love them and all others fiercely.

Be Bold

Take up space. Let the world know your name. Refuse to shrink back. Refuse to step aside. Refuse to apologize for existing. You are not sorry; you are certain. You know what you want to say. You know where you want to go. You know what you want to do with this one precious life that you have been given. Be your own kind of bold. Be your own brand of brave.

Take Risks Worth Taking

Know when to take risks and leap with fire and fury. Pursue the things that matter most in your life, even if they are not a guarantee. Trade monotony for spontaneity, at least every once in a while. Cross a few items off your bucket list. Be honest about what you want. Bet on yourself. Go after your dreams. Risk it all for love. Embrace the potential of failure over a life unlived.

Don't Wait for Permission

You do not need anyone else's permission to move through this world in pursuit of your purpose. You are not beholden to the opinions of those who are not going where you're going or have not been where you have been. You do not need to bend over backward to earn the approval of people who you wouldn't go to for advice. You don't have to prove your place or demonstrate your readiness to anyone. If you spend your life waiting for other people's permission to go after what you want, you will never begin.

Be True to Yourself

Don't change yourself to make people like you. Don't sacrifice your soul to earn their approval. Be true to yourself. You are enough. You are worthy. Remember that you are not defined by their opinions. People will try to slap their labels on you, try to push you into the roles that make them most comfortable. They may wield their words like weapons and make you change for their approval. Resist. Hold the line. Do not falter. The most important opinion of you is the one that you have of yourself. Honor that.

Rebel When Required

This rule is wholeheartedly inspired by the civil rights activist and late congressman John Lewis, who said, "Get in good trouble." In the end, sometimes it is not us who must change but the systems that force us to be anything less than who we are called to be. It is the unfair expectations rooted in antiquated power structures that must be ripped out like the weeds that they are. Pull them up. Tear them out. Burn them down. Remember that even miracle makers flip tables now and again.

Build Up or Shut Up

This rule is courtesy of my friend James Witty, who once mentioned this to me, and I loved it so much that I debated getting a tattoo of it on my body.

It's a fiery way of saying, "Use your words to build others up." Never underestimate the power of your voice. Know the potential impact it holds and use it accordingly. Do not tear others down. Champion the success of those around you. Be a reason others believe in themselves. Be a giver in a sea of takers. Be a builder in a world of demolition. Use your power to empower others. Use your gifts to leave a positive impact.

Stay Gutsy

Make a choice to be a little more courageous today than you were yesterday. Repeat this commitment tomorrow and the day after that. Remember that self-acceptance is a courageous act. Begin there. Grow from there. Uncover the bold and boundless bravery within you. March onward.

Now it's your turn. What are your rules to live by? What are the rules you will follow heading into the future to empower you to live your most gutsy life?

Write them down. Pin them to your bulletin board. Jot them onto sticky notes and add them to your bathroom mirror. Design a digital version of your rules and make it your computer or phone wallpaper.

Once you rewrite the rules of your life, the next step is living them. One hour, one day, one week at a time. Bring your rules into the forefront of your mind visually. Take action on them intentionally. Watch your world change.

What are the rules you desire to live by?

CONCLUSION

A few years ago, while I was getting prepped to go under anesthesia for brain surgery, a pang of panic hit me. Everything felt out of my control. Surgical prep felt like it was unfolding too quickly.

I just wanted more time.

I wasn't ready for the sweet exhaustion that weighed heavily on my eyes to pull me under. I wanted just a little longer as I held on to my husband's hand, not ready to be wheeled back into the operating room.

And in that moment of trepidation, a painful thought came barreling to the forefront of my mind…"I wonder if this is how so many people feel at the end of it all. Wishing that they had more time. Feeling that gentle slip from consciousness and realizing how much of their lives they never actually spent living."

The thought wrecked me.

Even saying it now wrecks me.

In that moment, I reflected on my own life and all the moments that I had spent trying to outrun my fears or hide from my insecurities or avoid doing anything that could cause me embarrassment or shame. I thought about all the time I had let slip by as I retreated back into myself—scrolling and scrolling and scrolling to avoid dealing with the pain of the past or the uncertainty of the future. In that moment, there was only one thing that kept running through my mind.

I wanted more time.

And yet time is the very thing that we can never get more of. It is the very thing that we can never get back. I wanted more time, and yet I realized that I wasn't promised a minute of it. It was all borrowed, and I had spent so much of my life naive to that fact.

In the years since my realization, I have shared this story repeatedly with many people that I meet. Many of them have stories like this of their own—a challenging diagnosis, losing someone they love, a close call, or an enduring struggle that reminds them of just how precious our time on this earth truly is. All of us with different stories, but we're all bound together by a shared realization of how fleeting and finite these moments truly are.

I know this is a hard realization. It is heavy. It runs deep. There is a large part of me that would very much prefer to avoid talking about it. However, I also know in my bones that to leave this lesson out of the story would be to deny you the very honesty that I promised at the start.

I would be remiss if in a book about courage, I failed to

confront the very thing that scares me most of all as a human being.

What scares me most...is running out of time.

I realized it that day heading into the operating room. Perhaps that fear had always existed, but that moment crystalized it for me.

With 100 percent certainty, I realized that my greatest fear is running out of time with the people that I love—running out of time to experience all the beauty that this world has to offer. Friends, that is the thing that keeps me up at night.

I think perhaps it is because it became clear in those moments before my surgery that I had been so careless with time in the past. I wouldn't go as far as to say I wasted it, but I certainly didn't value it like I should have.

I spent so much time worrying and so little time living... worrying about what other people thought of me, endlessly striving for their approval and looking outside myself for validation. There were so many things I never did, so many things I never said, out of fear of other people's opinions.

I let so much of my time slip away—barely lived in, barely touched. It was as if I felt like a passive participant in my own life, and I absolutely despised that feeling. I wanted more time.

The truth is that we always think there will be more of it. We always think that we can cling to the very thing that is unpredictably fleeting and always disappearing through our fingers.

We spend so many of our precious moments trying to

outrun the hard parts of our existence or avoiding what we fear the future might hold, and we end up losing the opportunity to truly experience the miracles all around us...even the miracle that lives within us.

Just in case no one has told you lately, please let me remind you...

You are a living miracle.

Born of stardust and floating through the infinite expanse of space and time, you exist in this precise sliver of existence with immense purpose. The alignment of every moment for generation upon generation for you to come into the world is astounding. You were created to make an impact on this world that only you can make.

Your heart beats. Air fills your lungs. Electricity pulses through the neurons firing in your brain. Your body does all of this without you even having to think about it. The magnitude of that alone is earth-shattering.

One single thing out of place in the millennia preceding this moment and there is a chance that you might not have even existed. The probability of you even being born is a number so small it is impossible to adequately comprehend it.

You are a living miracle. It is by no accident that you are here.

You have been given this one precious life, sweet friend. How are you going to spend it?

Every morning when you open your eyes, you have a decision to make. Will you rise to meet the day that awaits you?

Will you live the very miracle of a life that you have been given? I hope that you do.

I hope that regardless of what you have endured or what fears sit in front of you, you choose to make the most of every precious second.

I hope you keep fighting for all that is good and beautiful in this world. I hope you offer yourself the grace and forgiveness that you deserve, that you relinquish the pain of your past without carrying even an ounce of it with you into your future.

I hope you surround yourself with people who encourage, inspire, challenge, and empower you to become the best version of yourself. I hope you welcome the opinions of others from a place of confidence in who you are and what values you hold. I hope you do not allow the fear of their criticism and judgment to hold you back. I hope that you accept and love the person that you are underneath it all.

You are deserving of all of that...and so much more.

Today is the day that you step up to the mirror and see yourself with new eyes. Remember that self-acceptance is indeed a courageous act. Start by acknowledging who you are and what you earnestly want from your life; be vulnerable with yourself even if it requires a heap of bravery. Sometimes being honest with ourselves is the most courageous thing that we can do, after all.

Embrace that, to some degree, you will always care a little about what other people think of you. This is a feature and not a bug. It is how your brain is wired. However, you must be the one to redirect your attention away from what scares you and toward what you want from life.

Everyone is going to have an opinion, and they are entitled to it. However, you cannot allow other people's views of you to outweigh your view of yourself. Your voice must be the loudest one in your head. Your core values must guide you forward as the compass of your life.

Understand whose opinions matter and whose do not. Clarify who is a part of your inner circle. Ensure you receive feedback from a diverse group of sources, and open yourself to critical input when it comes from someone you trust.

Crank up the volume of your inner voice. Turn negative thought patterns into positive ones that propel you forward rather than hold you back. Build up your self-esteem. Nurture a healthy view of yourself. Affirm your strengths and ground yourself in the truth. Work to become so confident in who you are that what others think of you does very little to shake your self-perception.

Be confident in your ability to make decisions—even hard ones. Acknowledge when you feel stuck or stagnant and take one small step at a time until you gain the momentum you need to emerge victorious. Reframe your perception of failure. Bring play back into your life and take the pressure off when possible. Interrupt patterns that have been holding you hostage. Break free. Try something new.

Be willing to take risks. Raise your hand. Become an

engaged participant in your own life, and have the courage to suck at things. Do something you love, even if you are terrible at it. Remember that you do not need to be the best. You don't even need to be good. You are allowed to suck, and the world won't end if you do.

When you go out and get gutsy, at some point you are going to make a fool of yourself or let other people down. That is okay. It is an inevitable part of life. Just ensure that if you must disappoint someone, that person isn't yourself. Make yourself proud and remember who you are.

The truth is that you are the only one who holds the keys to the rest of your life—the only one who can unlock your heart to experience the fullness of what this world has to offer. You cannot change what people think of you or how they will react to you, but you can control you: your thoughts, your actions, your response to the situations around you.

In a world where there is much we cannot control, we must appreciate and take advantage of the things that we can. What you believe about yourself matters far more than what other people believe about you.

If you have been told you are too much, keep talking.

If you have been shamed for being bossy, keep leading.

If you have been deemed too difficult, never stop speaking the truth.

You can rewrite the rules. You can define how you measure success. Honor your needs. Have an opinion. Love your neighbor. Be bold. Take risks worth taking. Don't wait for permission. Be true to yourself. Rebel when required. Build up or shut up.

You are the only one who can release yourself from the prison of other people's opinions. You hold the key. You have the power to set yourself free.

Rise up and move forward with bold and boundless courage. Set down the weight of the world's expectations. Lay down the "shoulds" of it all. Quit obsessing over milestones that were never meant for you. Stop comparing yourself to everyone else. Simply be. Exist. Be proud of who you are and what you have overcome.

Today could be the first day of the rest of your life. Get up, get after it, and get gutsy.

Before We Say Farewell

I am not a fan of goodbyes. Never have been and never will be. And while I cannot wait to connect with you beyond the pages of this book, I want to leave you with one final resource to help you live a more courageous life. Are you in?

As we close out this book, I want to encourage you to take time to write a personal gutsy manifesto about who you are and what you love about yourself. Share your core values. Write about what makes you remarkable, strong, brave, and authentically you. Weave in the rules you live by. Embrace how you hope success will feel. Store it in a place for your future self to read when you are struggling.

I love a good manifesto. What can I say? They have always spoken to me. It serves as a dose of motivation that you can lean on when things get tough.

If you are a parent, consider having your kids write their own version of a personal manifesto as a positive exercise in self-esteem building. This can look like a list of affirmations or a guiding set of principles that they can recite as needed.

Manifestos can take many shapes and sizes—just as there is no single definition of success, there is no single right way to craft your own. Start writing and see where it leads you.

If you need a little inspiration to get you started, or if you want a manifesto you can build upon, I've got you covered. Consider this our collective rallying cry. It belongs to you just as much as it belongs to me. It is our gutsy anthem. I hope you like it.

A Gutsy Manifesto

The cynics and critics who taunt from the sidelines may see what stands before us, but they cannot fathom the courage that lies within us. With hopeful hands and healing hearts, we choose to honor the beauty of our imperfections.

No longer will we hide who we are or cower in the presence of other people's opinions. The weight of the world's expectations was heavy so we put it down. We let it go. We surrender the war we have been waging against ourselves and choose instead to open our hearts.

With self-assurance as our shield, core values as our compass, and a sword made from bold and boundless bravery, we march. Step by step we climb from the valley of validation and ascend to the summit where our striving ceases.

Here, we do not shrink back or dim our light. Here, we shine. Here, we allow ourselves to be seen, and we lift our voices to be heard. We look into the mirror bravely, and we commit to defend the bright soul we see staring back.

We choose to know ourselves, be ourselves, and love ourselves.

We hold space for our healing. We give grace in our grieving.

We are the compassionate caretakers of our inner child.

We do not run from what scares us. We run toward what fuels us.

Our purpose ignites us. Our passion fans the flames.

We are risk-takers, wave makers, and world changers.

We are the ones who dare to dream, the ones who choose to act.

We are brave. We are free. We are gutsy.

ACKNOWLEDGMENTS

There are more people to thank than I could ever possibly fit into the last few pages of this book. Behind every author is a community of people helping them go after their dreams. Thank you to everyone who has helped me get to where I am today.

To my husband, Hugh. You believed in me and in this book long before a word had ever been written. Thank you for every sacrifice, every word of encouragement, every hour of keeping our world together while I poured my heart onto the page. None of this would have been possible without you. The way you fight for my dreams as if they were your own is the thing of legends. I love you so much and I always will.

To Huey and Harlow. You are the reason I wrote this book. Thank you for teaching me every single day to live a life of bold, brave, and boundless courage.

To Carissa Ervin. You have become a part of our family over the past two years, and I am indebted to you for every hour you have spent caring for my babies. Thank you for loving my children as if they were your own.

To our Rising Tide leaders of the past seven years. You

are the leaders that I wish I had when I started. You give me one heck of a reason to be gutsy and fight for the independent business community that we love so dearly. Thank you for all that you do.

To my HoneyBook family. Your support over the past seven years has transformed tens of thousands of lives—including mine. Thank you for believing in me and for the work that you do every day to help others build a life of passion and purpose.

To the small but mighty NF team, past and present—thank you from the bottom of my heart for all of your support.

To my literary agents Karen, Curtis, and the entire Yates & Yates team—thank you for launching my writing career and believing in me from day one. I wouldn't be where I am today without your steadfast support.

To the Worthy Publishing and Hachette team. Thank you for bringing this book to life. To Beth for every hour you spent in the editing trenches and in countless meetings advocating for *Gutsy*. I am so grateful for you.

To Jess O'Leary. You are the friend I always prayed I would find one day. Thank you for loving me for who I am. There is so much of you infused into the pages of this book... which shouldn't be surprising. You are one of the most courageous women that I know.

To Black Market Bakers and Bread and Butter Kitchen. Thank you for keeping me fed and caffeinated during all of my writing weekends. Steve, I still cannot believe you played my first audiobook in the kitchen for everyone to hear. You rock. Thanks for always cheering for me. Monica, your courage makes our community better. I admire your guts and your giant heart.

To the infertility warriors who taught me so much about the true meaning of community. Your courage made me brave. To Kristin Gulitz, Ruth Hirata, and Ashley Yantes—you are extraordinary.

To my family. Mom, thank you for everything. You taught me what it means to be gutsy. When I think of courage, I always think of you. To my sister, Caroline. You jumped in the goal and never looked back. The way you approach life has always inspired me. I love you.

To Mom-Mom for teaching me what it means to make myself proud. I love you and miss you every single day. To my grandfather, Frank Pipkin, for buying two dozen copies of my first book and mailing them to all of your Naval Academy friends. My hand grew tired from signing all those copies, but I have never felt more loved. To my dad, Robin; my stepmother, Monica; and my little brother, Conor—I love you all so much. To my incredible in-laws, Melissa and Hugh, thank you for consistently and repeatedly going the extra mile to support my dreams and our family. To the entire Pipkin and Hayes crew—you are the bravest bunch I know. Thank you for cheering for me and this book every step of the way.

And most importantly, to Jesus. My greatest hope is that throughout my life and my work, I walk in Your footsteps. Love in action. Love for all.

ABOUT THE AUTHOR

Natalie Franke is an author, community builder, neuroscience nerd, and mama bear for small business. As one of the founders of the Rising Tide and the chief evangelist at HoneyBook, she supports over a hundred thousand independent business owners while fostering a spirit of community over competition around the world.

Natalie currently lives in Annapolis, Maryland, with her husband and two children. She's into doodling, drinking more caffeine than is appropriate, and giving bear hugs.